MW01484636

북 에 서 온 시 들

POEMS OF THE
NORTH

BAEK SEOK
백 석 시 모 음 집

EXILE PRESS 2018
KOREAN POETS SERIES
KOREANPOETS.ORG

exile press

북 에 서 온 시 들
POEMS OF THE NORTH

BAEK SEOK
백 석 시 모 음 집

Copyright © 2018 by Peter Liptak

Ordering Information: Special discounts available on quantity purchases by corporations, universities, and associations for sales promotions, premiums, fundraising, gifts and educational use. For details, contact info@exilepress.com

Exile Press
2355 Fairview Ave N #191
Roseville, MN 55113
www.exilepress.com

Baek Seok: Poems of the North / Baek Seok; Translated by Peter N Liptak
백석 시 모음집: 북에서 온 시들
ISBN: 978-89-962405-4-9 [Korea]   978-1-936342-09-9 [USA]
       978-1-936342-10-5 [ebook]   978-1-936342-84-6 [audiobook]
Library of Congress Control Number: 2018903310
p. 324 cm.21.6
First Edition
Printed in South Korea

Baek Seok: Poems of the North was published with the support of the Literature Translation Institute of Korea.

Exile Press 2018
Korean Poets Series
www.exilepress.com

exile press

Dedicated to Professor Yu Jong Ho
who introduced me to Baek Seok as
"The Great Untranslatable Poet."

Challenge accepted!

.

Thanks also to the many people who helped bring this work to life: my friend Joongwon Choi, whose art brings added depth to the poems, my research assistants Seola Kwon, HoJae Lee, Kang Seok Cho, Youngjoo Lee, Myung Sook Kwak, Min Jeong Lee, and SH Han, as well as many friends including the staff at Seoul Pub (RIP), and my lovely wife, EunJu Lee for her constant support, encouragement and help.

Born July 1st, 1912 as 백기행 (白夔行) Baek Gi-haeng
Pen name 백석 (白石 also 白奭) Baek Seok

As a foundational poet of the early modernist movement, Baek Seok made a conscious choice to be different. He chose to set his poetry apart from that of his peers, distancing himself from factions of poets, from their political debates and from the center and source of most modern poets' inspiration: Seoul. While other poets addressed the newness of industrialization and the flavors of new foods and other delights flooding in from the outside world, Baek Seok immersed himself in the foods and flavors native to Korea.

Baek Seok seemed to crave neither a sense of belonging nor the fodder of fresh ideas pouring in from the West. He had studied in Japan, spent time in the depths of English literature and later learned Russian to translate the literature of the North, yet he was able to create poems independent of these influences with distinctly Korean material. Careful to never fall back on hopeless romanticism or the brazen symbolism of the French influenced modern-for-the-sake-of-modernism poets, or even the feeble needy self-pitying fatalism in which many in the milieu of the Japanese occupation were apt to wallow.

He drew influences from the surroundings of nature, writing pastoral poetry that tapped into the memories and han of the people[1] in a natural setting that emphasized the objects surrounding Koreans in their daily lives. The universals of food and farm and mountain and village and beasts, not mystic but common and not common but comfortable, all found familiarity in his poems' framework. Employing a borrowed landscape technique put into practice by traditional landscape artists to avoid the use of unnecessary artifice, he brought man closer to nature epitomizing the Korean ideals of intimacy and harmony with nature.

Baek Seok himself mirrored in his poetry his disdain for the topics and concerns of his fellow poets by refusing even the shared meal of their camaraderie and the mediocrity that might accompany it, shunning too that pedestrian element of city comforts in his daily life, which entailed for him a good measure of wanderlust in a search for freedom in the beauty of the some-time Korean world. It is through this uniqueness

---

1 Han (한) is a culturally embedded Korean word used to describe the angst that built up in the souls of the people through centuries of hardship.

of voice as well as his bold shunning of popular concepts in early modernism that he was able to make an important contribution to the development of modern Korean poetry prior to liberation in 1945.

Following Korea's liberation from the Japanese, the complexity of the situation on the peninsula put Baek Seok in a delicate position as he was critical of the split of North and South. The so-called liberation had instilled in him a deep sense of the importance of community and compelled him to propose the alternative of a unified Korea, but at that moment, his path had diverged from the current of the present milieu, so he was forced to resort to translation and set his poetic voice aside.

The end of the war prompted Baek Seok's return to literary activities with forays into children's poetry and fairy tales (not covered in this volume). He avoided advancing the ideas of revolution and class-consciousness, and his children's literature began instigating arguments as he criticized the "Socialist Roadmap" of North Korea's Children's literature.

In the postwar thaw between North and South, Baek Seok continued to assert his literary views and in the 1958 purge, was banished to a government-managed farming collective. In a farming village with no electricity, he lived a communal life and composed poems of imagery. In 1959, releasing *Eastern Restaurant*, which was reminiscent of *Family of Fox Valley* and his other early work:

> Children happy as a holiday
> in the yard playing tag, hide-and-seek
> on the wooden walkways the sound of chatter, the cackle's clatter
> the adults as if at a fair feeling festive
> the doorway, the main door open and shut successively in and out
> in the doorway, the main room explodes with laughter

This farm village helped him to regain a sense of communal life, but he soon became frustrated with the confines of socialism. By the end of 1962, he suffered a bitter blow from a storm of reactionary critics across North Korea, and so ceased his creative activities. From that time, his name disappeared from the annals of the literary world of North Korea. And though many speculated that Baek Seok passed away in 1995, further research of his family chronology revealed that he died in January of 1996.

> At some moment, to loose a wife and
> the house we made a life in
> and to be far from my frugal parents and siblings
> to wander aimless through the force of wind to the end of a
> lonesome lane···

and

> With time's passage, I realize I lack a wife and also
> Lost is the house of our mutual habitation...
> And my prudent parents and also my siblings fell to far off,
> To the end of this some strong winded lonely road, I wander'd about...

The late literary critic Kim, Hyeon chose Baek Seok's poem *Park Si-bong's Place* as the finest in modern literature (its opening above). Much like his life, this poem wanders endlessly. To him a field of falling snow was his home, every woman in the street, a sister. Baek Seok's use of folk language to express the profound sorrow and deep resentment of the people, is matched only by the work of Seo, JeongJu in the South.

Baek Seok's poems paint a timeless picture of the Korean countryside steeped in tradition, showing the Korean condition both current and past with a hint of the possibility for some return to that former greatness and peace in the future.

9

Peter Nicholas Liptak 情石 (정석)
Born May 22nd, 1969

After graduating from the University of Minnesota in English Literature, Peter Liptak came to Korea in 1995 where he lived and worked for 20 years. Finding in Seoul a source of inspiration, linguistic and otherwise, he began studying Korean at Ewha Woman's University and later at Seoul National University. Later, as cohost of the show Explore

Korea he gained a greater appreciation of the country and its history. A dearth of interesting study materials in the standard courses at the time led him to begin examining Korean poetry as a way of expanding his understanding of the language and people. A poet himself, Mr. Liptak discovered somthing akin to his own development in the early modernist movement of Korean poets, especially in the fervent times of the Japanese occupation and began an MA in Korean Studies at Yonsei University's Graduate School of International Studies where he was first introduced to the palatal poems of Baek Seok.

Mr. Liptak has penned more than thirty books as a poet, author, teacher and publisher, but continued to return to the simple beauty of Baek Seok's poetry and the slow process of decoding them. "When I resolved to tackle the task of translating Baek Seok's poems, I began the journey with the simple impetus of an appreciation of his work and wish to understand it, but more so due to some mysterious connection I felt to his writing style, a sort of jung[1] had developed that linked me to his work." After embarking on this journey, Mr. Liptak began to understand the depth of Baek Seok's contributions to the development of modern Korean poetry and the collective consciousness of the Korean condition overall.

Why Baek Seok?

This most Korean of Korean poets, his work both palatal and pastoral, shunning the new ideas and objects of the times in favor of those objects connected with Korean traditional life inspired Mr Liptak to delve deeper. The intense descriptions particularly poignant in relation to the backdrop of the Japanese occupation, the loss of Korea's nationhood

---

1 Jung (정) is an affection, closeness or bond that builds between people over time.

and with it much of its linguistic freedom and national character.

Baek Seok had remained in the North and when the war began in 1950 became sequestered in the minds of South Koreans as a 'writer who went north.'[1] His work became proscribed in the milieu of staunch anticommunist sentiments that dominated in the South after the Korean war. South Koreans were unable to access his poetry until 1988, his work was largely forgotten by the populace. In the North, the situation was similarly difficult for Baek Seok and his creative endeavors, as he had been forced to withdraw from writing and live out his remaining days as a farmer.

But in the final evaluation of this project's potential significance, with the current situation in North Korea one might easily overlook the long and proud history, culture and traditions of the region. It is the hope of Mr. Liptak that a brief glimpse at the people as they were, before the peninsula was torn in an ideological showdown, and as they are preserved in Baek Seok's poetry will bring new light to the eyes of those who would judge the people of the Koreas.

Baek Seok gives us a rare glimpse into the everyday lives of the common people. These people of the Korean peninsula now divided, but sharing a long history of tradition, together hold the heritage that is much overlooked when viewing Asian contributions to world culture. And as such, it is the translator's further hope that this publication may transmit a portion of that literary heritage on to the world community.

Perhaps it is from the present situation in which the world views North Korea that an evaluation of Baek Seok may do the most good. While

---

1 Wolbukchaka (월북작가) writers who went to the North were proscribed in the South.

so much of the press is focused Kim Jong Eun and the Juche System of the North, whether it be nuclear proliferation, the Military First tactics of Kim Jong-un's government, the dire situation of the economy, or invoking pity for the hunger of the masses, one might easily overlook the long and proud history, culture and traditions of the entire peninsula or judge the North Korean people (still wishfully refered to as "our northern brothers" by many in the South) by their government's actions or those who merely wish to understand what it is and was to be Korean.

The Journey Continues

An award winning poet and writer of children's books, Peter N. Liptak founded Exile Press and its imprints, Little Bear Books and Hungry Dictator Press with the mission of learning from beyond borders, from culture in communication, and from what we may discover from the microcosm of word's art and the exploration of the poetic voice.

In the fifteen years, it has taken to bring this volume of Baek Seok's work to fruition, Peter has authored several language acquisition books for learners of English and Korean, including his most popular work: As much as a Rat's Tail, a book introducing non-native speakers to the inner workings of Korean Slang. Working also for the Korean Government and other global organizations in Korea and abroad as a copywriter, he hopes to contribute to globalization within Korea and continue to promote Korean culture and literature to the outside world.

As a further goal, Exile Press plans to publish other works of outstanding Korean poets through it's Korean Poets Series and promote them on KoreanPoets.org

Abstract

The Palatal Poems of Baek Seok

"Any healthy man can go without food for two days
– but not without poetry."

Charles Baudelaire, (1821–1867)

Through poetry, Baek Seok was able to find such sustenance. As he
developed his craft, this North Korean poet from Pyungangbukdo
observed (and thereby helped to preserve) the institutions and character
of fading local customs by infusing them with foods and flavors
native to Korea, a deep and spiritual connection to the natural world,
and shamanic superstition. His rediscovery of the innate national

consciousness through repeated meditation and exploration of tradition, as an expression of historical consciousness, has allowed his poetry to take on a quality of ethnography.

Taking his influences from the visually intense landscape objects and narratives of the countryside, Baek Seok created pastoral poetry embedded in local traditions that tapped into the memories and han[1] of the people. The universals of food, farm, mountain, village and beasts, not mystic but common, and not common but comfortable, all found their familiarity in his poems' framework, while epitomizing the Korean ideals of intimacy and harmony with nature, employing a "borrowed landscape" technique put into practice by traditional landscape artists to avoid the use of unnecessary artifice, thereby bringing man closer to nature. And despite the intense dialect of his early poems, the form they took was grammatically simple making them easily readable. In essence, his choices of voice, style, vernacular and objects made him the most Korean of the Korean poets.

With a tone that is variously meditative, joyous, nostalgic, critical, romantic, reverent, ironic, tragic and even bitter at times, Baek Seok's blend of litany, landscape and legend is full of nature's color, readily palatal flavors of rural cookery and an "almost tactile connection to those who people the poems."[2] His poems paint a picture of the Korean countryside that is timeless in its application to her rich past of traditions, allowing us to experience his intense descriptions of a world now largely lost and to see into the culture and human relationships of the Korean condition.

1   Han (한) see page 7 footnote.
2   David R. McCann (Ed.), Columbia Anthology of Modern Korean Poetry, Columbia University Press (2004), translated by Kyunghwan Choi, p.84

Bringing a Taste of Koreanness to the Table of Modernism

In a land still unified, yet struggling for freedom with food shortages a constant reality, he treated his readers to the dishes they craved, making his poems particularly poignant in relation to the backdrop of the oppressive Japanese occupation. Providing a rare glimpse of the people and the objects that surrounded them, both inimitable and common, Baek Seok's poems exhibit a heritage not so much of the Korea as it was, mired in the reality of the period, but in the imagination of its greatness throughout history.

Baek Seok also composed poetry that lacked artifice and invoked concrete images of the Korean countryside with visually intense landscape objects and narratives. Through the combination of traditional material and modern style, he was able to create a new dish with a taste palatable to Koreans in the face of their loss of independence. While other poets like Yi Sang, Kim Ki Rim and Jung Ji Young wrote of the new foods, objects and experiences that the Japanese and western worlds brought to Korea's doorstep, Baek Seok treated his readers to a cornucopia of traditional tastes.

One of the outstanding features of Baek Seok's work is its folk character, recounting the customs and manners of common people from the pre-modern era and expressing an earnest devotion to Korean folk style in the voice of the modern citizenry. This method allows us to gain insight into the connection of people to their ethnic customs and cultural heritage, as with 'Family of Fox Valley' or 'Ancient Night,' and other poems that convey a sense of communal unity to the reader.

"...fighting over warm spots on the heated floor and giggling away sleep comes on the window the roof's awning casting a morning shadow the younger second aunties crowd the noisy kitchen through the side door's gap we sleep to the delicious seeping scent of salted shrimp-flavored Chinese radish soup simmering"

"A night like tomorrow's on the Harvest festival in the kitchen the intense fire bright, the pot's trembling lid a savory smell of beef marrow soup at a full boil, in the room great aunt came to tell village rumors while crafting each the half moon rice cakes and the full moon rice cakes and the acarus rice cakes and beside I taste the chestnut powder and red bean powder and sugary soybean powder and think the sugary soybean powder is the most delicious"

Yet the most remarkable characteristic remains his use of dialect as such dialectic conscious consciousness is unmatched in the annals of modern Korean poetry.

Much overlooked in their contributions to world culture, the long and proud history, culture and traditions of the region are embedded with an uncertainty related to North Korea's authoritative and imposing history, its veiled culture and the enigma of its people. Baek Seok provides for us a brief picture of the people as they were before the peninsula was torn. The objects he addressed were those items natural to Korea, often embedded in local traditions and familiar to the people of the countryside. He wrote poetry of, and ultimately for, the people without falling into the trap of proletarian literature, which most often lacked poetic depth as it attempted to force a moral message on its readers.

Finally, Baek Seok wrote in a modern poetic style that blazed a new path for Korean poetry while remaining true to the culture of an independent Korea and making an impact on the landscape of modern Korean poetry through his use of dialect, a child's voice, and shamanist elements, as well as the forgotten tastes and tongues of the North and all of Korea.

As others like Kim Ki Rim and Yi Sang created a new literature written in Hangul along European lines, Baek Seok sought to develop a genre unique to Korea full of the foods and landscapes he relished and remembered. His contribution to modernism in Korean poetry was broadening the scope of poetry on the peninsula by creating a discipline that was both Korean and modern at once. He set his own table in the field of modernism and was able invite the world to enjoy a truly Korean dish.

Writing in his mother tongue in a time where use of Korean in schools and publications was frowned upon by the Japanese cultural policy. While his poems could not easily be categorized as anti-Japanese in their tone, he expressly avoided touching on anything reminiscent of Japanese influence, systematically reflecting the dialect of the Kwanso Region. He appears to use dialect as a type of resistance to the standardized language of the period, illustrating the strength of Baek Seok's opposition to the modern centralization of power and its burgeoning materialism in the daily lives of real people durring the Japanese occupation.

This publication will examine Baek Seok's contribution to the landscape of Korean poetry in the modern era through his only published collection, entitled "Deer," in translation as well as his later works through liberation and up to the division of North from South.

Table of Contents

Deer
사슴

A Bovine Calf 's Call 얼룩소 새끼의 영각

Stone Mortar's Water 돌덜구의 물

The Roe 노루

Series Poems
연작시

The Heart's Wanderings
종잡을 수 없는 마음

The Palatal & Pastoral
맛과 향과 전원시

26

Fauna & Flora
동식물상

Manchu Poems
만주시

Deer 사슴

A Bovine Calf 's Call

얼룩소 새끼의 영각

Woman of Gajeurang[1]

Before where a coyote raised her cubs, the iron hammer-carrying
bandits would appear, Gajeurang pass

Gajeurang cottage, below the pass
From the village beyond the mountain, the night deprived of a sow,
chasing the beast a fearful beating gong's clang reached this place
A cottage where chickens, dogs and other domestics could not be
raised[2]
A cottage where wild boars as if close cousins would pass by

Past sixty, the childless old maid of Gajeurang, pure as a monk, if
she walks to the village, many long pipes of strong coarse tobacco are
offered up

Last night below the stone steps, the coyote came, such a tale
Somewhere in a secluded mountain district, a bear tends to a child,
the tale tells

As I eat steamed rice cakes with stonecrop kimchi [3]
As if by proverb in a spirit inhabited house, a mudang's dwelling[4]

---

1 The Jib (집) in Gajeurang Jib (가즈랑집) can also mean house, but here it refers to the
   woman of that house.

2 In Korea a mudang (무당), shaman, medium or exorcist, was prohibited from living with
   animals or people in order to preserve the purity of his or her spirit.

3 Stonecrop (돌나물), an annual or perennial flowering mountain herb with fleshy leaves,
   native to northern temperate regions, is often used to make kimchi. Genus: Sedum

4 A god's daughter (구신집), or mudang, is a female practitioner of shamanism who acts
   as an intermediary between the ancestral or natural spirits, supernatural forces, or gods
   and the human plain through 'gut' or rituals, reminiscent of exorcism, to tell fortunes,
   cure illness, bring good luck, or repulse evil spirits.

The woman of Gajeurang

When I emerged, also when my now dead sister was born,

She wrote our names on a roll of cotton cloth, closed with baekji[5]

and enclosed it in a wicker basket on the spirit ledge to be adopted by

his Excellency, the woman of Gajeurang

Every time I suffer from disease,

It's the spirit king's persecution, declares the woman of Gajeurang

When I think of her, the spirit daughter, I am saddened

When the rabbit is said to fatten, down in the mire gathering wild

edible greens and fragrant grasses, fernbrake, valerian, iron fern, wild

aster, royal fern, bracken, Japanese angelica, and buds, I followed the

woman of Gajeurang

I already think of sugary sweet soaked squill roots and simmered

Solomon's seals and

Yearn for the yet far off acorn jelly and thick acorn porridge

Behind the house under the plum tree, as I seek a newly fallen plum

A lightning plum struck and she watched me cry and smile

Let's see how many feet[6] of hair has sprouted from your bottom,[7]

the woman of Gajeurang

While eating a new peach, choking down the pit was like dying so

the whole day I could not play or eat

Going to visit Gajeurang cottage

Delighting like a puppy fed with a rice liquor remnant, I fluttered in

and out

5   Baekji (백지) is a strip of white paper often hung on cairns for luck.

6   A Korean foot, or cha (자) is 30.3cm.

7   Hair sprouting from one's bottom (밑구멍에 털이 몇 자나 났나) is a Korean idiomatic
    expression for growing older.

가즈랑집

승냥이가 새끼를 치는 전에는 쇠메 든 도적이 났다는 가즈랑고개

가즈랑집은 고개 밑의
산(山) 너머 마을서 도야지를 잃는 밤 짐승을 쫓는 깽제미 소리가 무서웁게
들려 오는 집
닭 개 짐승을 못 놓는
멧도야지와 이웃사촌을 지나는 집

예순이 넘은 아들 없는 가즈랑집 할머니는 중같이 정해서 할머니가 마을을
가면 긴 담뱃대에 독하다는 막써레기를 몇 대라도 붙이라고 하며

간밤에 섬돌 아래 승냥이가 왔었다는 이야기
어느메 산(山) 골에선간 곰이 아이를 본다는 이야기

나는 돌나물김치에 백설기를 먹으며
옛말의 구신집에 있는 듯이
가즈랑집 할머니
내가 날 때 죽은 누이도 날 때
무명필에 이름을 써서 백지 달아서 구신간시렁의 당즈깨에 넣어 대감님께
수영을 들였다는 가즈랑집 할머니

언제나 병을 앓을 때면
신장님 단련이라고 하는 가즈랑집 할머니
구신의 딸이라고 생각하면 슬퍼졌다

토끼도 살이 오른다는 때 아르대즘퍼리에서 제비꼬리 마타리 쇠조지
가지취 고비 고사리 두릅순 회순 산(山) 나물을 하는 가즈랑집 할머니를
따르며

나는 벌써 달디단 물구지우림 둥굴네우림을 생각하고
아직 멀은 도토리묵 도토리범벅까지도 그리워한다

뒤울안 살구나무 아래서 광살구를 찾다가
살구벼락을 맞고 울다가 웃는 나를 보고
밑구멍에 털이 몇 자나 났나 보자고 한 것은 가즈랑집 할머니다
찰복숭아를 먹다가 씨를 삼키고는 죽는 것만 같아 하루종일 놀지도 못하고
밥도 안 먹은 것도
가즈랑집에 마을을 가서
당세 먹은 강아지같이 좋아라고 집오래를 설레다가였다

Family of Fox Valley

As I followed mama and papa, our house-dog followed me on the national holiday we went to great grandparents house

Her face pockmarked with star prints, blinking with speech, all day weaving a bolt of hemp cloth, past the house with many peach trees in Shinri, that auntie, auntie's daughters the Lee lass and little Lee lass

At sixteen, the over forty widower's second wife to become, blue-faced and easily angered with lips the russet of water that boiled fermented soybeans and nipples darker still near the Jesus Believers' village living in Tosan village, that auntie, auntie's daughter Seung lass and son Seung lad

They say sixty li[1] past the bluish looking mountain at the beach, widowed with red tipped nose always wearing white at conversations end often wringing sad tears, that big village auntie, auntie's daughter Hong lass, sons Hong lad and little Hong lad

Able at pear tree splicing pulling out stone steps when drunk skilled at setting duck snares enjoying the journey to some distant island to salt large-eyed herring, that uncle, uncle's mother, eldest sister and the younger cousins

These chock-full relations, with grandma and grandpa together in the inner room sensing the smell of new clothes

Also with the smell of injolmi,[2] pine flavored rice cakes, bean powdered rice cakes and the meal's tofu and bean sprouts and fried grass and fernbrake and pork-fat all with a sudden shivering chill of

---

1   A li (리) is a traditional Korean unit of distance that has varied over time, but is roughly 0.4-0.5km or about a third of a mile. Sixty li would be about 24 km.

2   Injeolmi (인절미) is a glutinous rice cake, a chewy mugwort ddeok coated with soybean powder.

cold shock

The children lay down their dinner rice spoons and beside the barn near the inner garden, on the pear tree hill chase mice and play hide-and-seek and grab-the-tail and bride-to-be sedan chair ride and groom's horse ride like this play bustling into the dark night

As the night grows darker in the house the mothers in their inner rooms laugh and giddily talk, the children amongst themselves in outer rooms play jackstones and dice-cubes and spin lids circus-like and play let-go-the-pumpkin[3] and a hand-in-hand swallow song game and like this through a number of times raising the lantern's wick the morning rooster crying a number of times drowsing fighting over warm spots on the heated floor and giggling away sleep comes on the window the roof's awning casting a morning shadow the younger second aunties crowd the noisy kitchen through the side door's gap we sleep to the delicious seeping scent of salted shrimp-flavored Chinese radish soup simmering

3 Let-go-the-pumpkin (호박떼기) is a game, presumably similar to "hot-potato."

여우난골족

　명절날 나는 엄매 아배 따라 우리집 개는 나를 따라 진할머니
진할아버지가 있는 큰집으로 가면

　얼굴에 별자국이 솜솜 난 말수와 같이 눈도 껌적거리는 하루에 베 한
필을 짠다는 벌 하나 건너 집엔 복숭아나무가 많은 신리(新里) 고무 고무의
딸 이녀(李女) 작은 이녀(李女) 열여섯에 사십(四十)이 넘은 홀아비의 후처가
된 포족족하니 성이 잘 나는 살빛이 매감탕 같은 입술과 젖꼭지는 더 까만
예수쟁이 마을 가까이 사는 토산(土山) 고무 고무의 딸 승녀(承女)아들
승(承)동이
　육십리(六十里)라고 해서 파랗게 뵈이는 산을 넘어 있다는 해변에서 과부가
된 코끝이 빨간 언제나 흰옷이 정하든 말 끝에 섧게 눈물을 짤 때가 많은 큰골
고무 고무의 딸 홍녀(洪女) 아들 홍(洪)동이 작은 홍(洪)동이
　배나무접을 잘 하는 주정을 하면 토방돌을 뽑는 오리치를 잘 놓는 먼섬에
반디젓 담그러 가기를 좋아하는 삼춘 엄매 사춘누이 사춘 동생들이 그득히들
할머니 할아버지가 있는 안간에들 모여서 방안에서는 새옷의 내음새가 나고
　또 인절미 송구떡 콩가루차떡의 내음새도 나고 끼때의 두부와 콩나물과
뽂운 잔디와 고사리와 도야지비계는 모두 선득선득하니 찬 것들이다

저녁술을 놓은 아이들은 외양간섶 밭마당에 달린 배나무 동산에서
쥐잡이를 하고 숨굴막질을 하고 꼬리잡이를 하고 가마타고 시집가는 놀음 말
타고 장가가는 놀음을 하고 이렇게 밤이 어둡도록 북적하니 논다
　밤이 깊어가는 집안엔 엄매는 엄매들끼리 아르간에서들 웃고 이야기하고
아이들은 아이들끼리 웃간 한 방을 잡고 조아질하고 쌈방이 굴리고
바리깨돌림하고 호박떼기하고 제비손이구손이하고 이렇게 화디의
사기방등에 심지를 몇 번이나 돋구고 홍게닭이 몇번이나 울어서 졸음이
오면 아릇목싸움 자리싸움을 하며 히드득 거리다 잠이 든다 그래서는
문창에 텅납새의 그림자가 치는 아침 시누이 동세들이 욱적하니 흥성거리는
부엌으론 샛문틈으로 장지 문틈으로 무이징게국을 끓이는 맛있는 내음새가
올라오도록 잔다

The Storeroom

In the old clay pot, like the aging married daughter unable to return,[1]
the pine flavored rice cakes lasted a length[2]

In the glazed jar, was the makgeolli my uncle enjoyed more than
eating[3]
Mimicking him, my cousin and I consistently snatched the sourish
puckery pleasing liquor

Every Memorial Day, beside our deaf grandfathers, we cracked giant
chestnuts and pierced tofu kebabs with bush clover skewers

As the grandchildren gather like flies, a bear paw like hand faithfully
shoos them away

On the corner wall rack, the cow-sized straw sandals grandfather
had woven were well hung, heaped high

Behind the rice bin of the dark storeroom where legends live on,
even with the call for dinner I pretended not to hear

---

1 The Korean here (갈 줄 모르는) implies 'to her husband's home.'

2 Songgu ddok (송구떡) or pine rice cakes are typically eaten during the Tano Festival.

3 Chapssal takju (찹쌀탁주) is a type of makgeolli (raw or unrefined milky-white wine)
made from glutinous rice or wheat mixed with nuruk (a fermentation starter).

고방

낡은 질동이에는 갈 줄 모르는 늙은 집난이같이 송구떡이 오래도록 남아
있었다

오지항아리에는 삼촌이 밥보다 좋아하는 찹쌀탁주가 있어서
삼촌의 임내를 내어가며 나와 사춘은 시큼털털한 술을 잘도채어 먹었다

제삿넬이면 귀머거리 할아버지 가에서 왕밤을 밝고 싸리꼬치에 두부산적을
께었다

손자아이들이 파리떼같이 모이면 곰의 발 같은 손을 언제나내어 둘렀다

구석의 나무말쿠지에 할아버지가 삼는 소신 같은 짚신이 둑둑이 걸리어도
있었다

옛말이 사는 컴컴한 고방의 쌀독 뒤에서 나는 저녁끼때에 부르는 소리를
듣고도 못 들은 척하였다

The Bonfire

Even a bit of rope, even a spent shoe, even cow dung, even a torn horsehair hat, even dog's teeth, even a length of plank, even dried straw, even fallen leaves, even a lock of hair, even a ripped rag, even a skewer stick, even a roof tile, even a hen's feather, even a dog's coat, amid the bonfire burn

Even a distant relation, even a Yangban scholar,[1] even a patriarch, even an indigent child, even a new son-in-law, even a recent marriage relation, even a wayfarer, even a landlord, even a grandfather, even a grandchild, even a seller of writing brushes, even a tinsmith, even a great dog, even a puppy, all take warmth at the bonfire

Within the bonfire, my grandfather in youth without his ma n' pa as a somber boy piteously orphaned, such is his sad history

1   A yangban scholar, using the old choshi (초시) here, is a Korean aristocrat.

모닥불

새끼오리도 헌신짝도 소똥도 갓신창도 개니빠디도 너울쪽도 짚검불도
가락잎도 머리카락도 헝겊 조각도 막대꼬치도 기왓장도 닭의 깃도 개터럭도
타는 모닥불

재당도 초시도 문장(門長) 늙은이도 더부살이 아이도 새사위도 갓사둔도
나그네도 주인도 할아버지도 손자도 붓장사도 땜쟁이도 큰개도 강아지도 모두
모닥불에 쪼인다

모닥불은 어려서 우리 할아버지가 어미아비 없는 서러운 아이로
불상하니도 몽둥발이가 된 슬픈 역사가 있다

Ancient Night

Papa went to a foreign land not returning, on a remote steep
mountain slope only the two of us mama and me such a scary night as
if to kill us from the backyard from some mountain valley came the
sound of cattle-grabbing good-for-nothings slaughtering a cow[1] for
anju as if thieving bastards thump-thumping around

Grabbing the straw mat drying grain kicking and rolling, the
nana who raised chickens under the ground of the whale-like tiled
house always with bean flour coated rice cakes and honey and full
of silver'n'gold treasure, a one-legged Chomagu[2] somewhere on the
mountain back Chomagu exists waking in the deep night to piss at the
window frame above my head, the soldier Chomagu's deep black head
and deep black eyeballs gaze in then I cringe and cower under my
blanket shrink and hide unable to rest

Again such a time of night my young maiden aunt, about to marry,
passed the hill came to the family head's home bearing adorning fabric
and with mama the pair to the light of two lit cow-oil wicks into the
night sewing that time of night, near the fire I carried a reed mat and
took out dried chestnuts long withered like a squirrel to strip and eat
and with an ironing spoon, toast and eat the fruit of a gingko, even so
above the blanket I do a circus act and also lie and roll to mama away
from the fire's heat the extended folding screen's bright red magic

---

1   In this period, one must gain permission from the government to slaughter cattle or pigs
    and these 'low-level' men often do it secretly in the night for anju (안주), which are side
    dishes eaten while drinking alcohol.
2   An old tale tells of an incredibly short midget called Chomagu (조마구).

peach story, I even listened to and on a clear day demanded auntie
over and over to catch a quail that cannot fly far

A night like tomorrow's on the Harvest festival in the kitchen
the intense fire bright, the pot's trembling lid a savory smell of beef
marrow soup at a full boil, in the room great aunt came to tell village
rumors while crafting each the half moon rice cakes and the full moon
rice cakes and the acarus rice cakes[3] and beside I taste the chestnut
powder and red bean powder and sugary soybean powder and think
the sugary soybean powder is the most delicious
How much I had wanted to work with the dough my hands made
white no one could know
On the last day of the last month, that last night if snow will fall in
the night an utter white aged woman's spirit and a snow specter too
cannot fly out to catch the last snow as I firmly believe this story ma
and me at the fire hole on the rice cake stone on the wall propped up
by a wooden bowl placed a great brass bowl to earnestly pray for a last
snow, a healing snow to obtain the thawed snow, the last water they
say to fill a prayer bottle, a tribute pot to pass the year with water to
use when colds come and bellies ache and we suffer colic

3 Acarus, or juin-du-gi (쥔두기) is a flour mite, so acarus rice cakes are shapes like mites.

고야(古夜)

아배는 타관 가서 오지 않고 산비탈 외따른 집에 엄매와 나와 단둘이서
누가 죽이는 듯이 무서운 밤 집 뒤로는 어느 산골짜기에서 소를 잡어먹는
노나리꾼들이 도적놈들같이 쿵쿵거리며 다닌다

날기멍석을 져간다는 닭보는 할미를 차 굴린다는 땅 아래 고래 같은 기와
집에는 언제나 니차떡에 청밀에 은금보화가 그득하다는 외발 가진 조마구
뒷산 어느메도 조마구네 나라가 있어서 오줌 누러 깨는 재밤 머리맡의 문살에
대인 유리창으로 조마구 군병의 새까만 대가리 새까만 눈알이 들여다보는 때
나는 이불 속에 자즐어붙어 숨도 쉬지 못한다

또 이러한 밤 같은 때 시집갈 처녀 막내 고무가 고개 너머 큰집으로
치장감을 가지고 와서 엄매와 둘이 소기름에 쌍심지의 불을 밝히고 밤이
들도록 바느질을 하는 밤 같은 때 나는 아릇목의 삿귀를 들고 쇠든밤을
내여 다람쥐처럼 발거먹고 은행여름을 인두불에 구어도 먹고 그러는 이불
위에서 광대넘이를 뒤이고 또 누어 굴면서 엄매에게 웃목에 두른 평풍의
새빨간 천두의 이야기를 듣기도 하고 고무더러는 밝는 날 멀리는 못 난다는
뫼추라기를 잡어달라고 조르기도 하고

내일같이 명절날인 밤은 부엌에 쩨듯하니 불이 밝고 솥뚜껑이 놀며
구수한 내음새 곰국이 무르끓고 방안에서는 일가집 할머니가 와서 마을의
소문을 펴며 조개송편에 달송편에 송편에 떡을 빚는 곁에서 나는 밤소 팥소
설탕 든 콩가루소를 먹으며 설탕 든 콩가루소가 가장 맛있다고 생각한다
나는 얼마나 반죽을 주무르며 흰가루손이 되여 떡을빚고 싶은지 모른다
섣달에 내빌날이 들어서 내빌날 밤에 눈이 오면 이 밤엔 쌔하얀 할미귀신의
눈귀신도 내빌눈을 받노라 못난다는 말을 든든히 여기며 엄매와 나는 앙궁
위에 떡돌 위에 곱새담 위에 함지에 버치며 대냥푼을 놓고 치성이나 드리듯이
정한 마음으로 내빌눈 약눈을 받는다 이 눈 세기물을 내빌물이라고 제주병에

진상항아리에 채워두고는 해를 묵여가며 고뿔이 와도 배앓이를 해도
갑피기를 앓어도 먹을 물이다

Duck Pony Hare

To set the duck snare, father left for the rice paddy long ago
The duck, its shadow falling on the hill slope, flies away,
On the levee, like a puppy as I call father and cry
My temper rises, so too the stream at my back, my father's shoes and
socks and pantleg ties, I cast them all out

On the morning of market day along the wide road in front, the
pony following its mother, let it stay with me I beg
Pa turns to the street and shouts
----- foaly come 'ere
----- foaly come 'ere

Going to chop wood, to put atop pa's coolie rack, I consider
catching hares as we head for the mountain

As I block the hare burrow's passageway, always the baby rabbits
scurry away under my legs
I, in my touched and tender state, gather a tearful semblance

오리 망아지 토끼

오리치를 놓으려 아배는 논으로 나려간 지 오래다
오리는 동비탈에 그림자를 떨어트리며 날아가고 나는 동말랭이에서
강아지처럼 아배를 부르며 울다가
시악이 나서는 등뒤 개울물에 아배의 신짝과 버선목과 대님오리를 모다
던져 버린다

장날 아츰에 앞 행길로 엄지 따러 지나가는 망아지를 내라고 나는 조르면
아배는 행길을 향해서 크다란 소리로
- 매지야 오나라
- 매지야 오나라

새하려 가는 아배의 지게에 지워 나는 산(山)으로 가며 토끼를 잡으리라고
생각한다

맞구멍난 토끼굴을 내가 막어서면 언제나 토끼새끼는 내 다리 아래로
달어났다
나는 서글퍼서 서글퍼서 울상을 한다

Stone Mortar's Water

돌덜구의 물

Early Winter Day

As the warm rays struck the earthen wall
The children sniveled as they ate sweet potatoes

A heavenly rain on the stone mortar cooled
Radish leaves dried aloft the peach tree

초동일 (初冬日)

흙담벽에 볕이 따사하니
아이들은 물코를 흘리며 무감자를 먹었다

돌덜구에 천상수(天上水)가 차게
복숭아나무에 시라리타래가 말러갔다

Summer Rice Paddy

As if mateless tits on tiptoe were the children poised
On the row's ridge as they roasted and feasted on frog legs

Poking at an open crawfish-hole, the muddy feeling's a captured
snake
The moss spread out red as blood about in the sun's hot rays

On a stone bridge seated amid a feast of raw minnows their bodies
drying in the sun
Transformed the children to kingfishers

하답 (夏沓)

  짝새가 발뿌리에서 날은 논드렁에서 아이들은 개구리의 뒷다리를 구어먹었다

  게구멍을 쑤시다 물쿤하고 배암을 잡은 늪의 피 같은물이끼에 햇볕이 따그웠다

  돌다리에 앉어 날버들치를 먹고 몸을 말리는 아이들은 물총새가 되었다

A Tavern

Wrapped in a pumpkin leaf, that boiled carp she brought was ever
appetizing

In the kitchen on that table, that brilliantly polished octagonal
serving table
One could see a bright blue bush clover painted on an eyeball-sized
glass

Her son, Bom, who caught minnows well, buck-toothed to boot,
was my same age

Outside the millet fence, a peddler was followed by the suckling
foal at its mother's breast

주막 (酒幕)

호박잎에 싸오는 붕어곰은 언제나 맛있었다

부엌에는 빨갛게 질들은 팔(八)모알상이 그 상 위엔 새파란 싸리를 그린
눈알만한 산(蓋)이 보였다

아들 아이는 범이라고 장고기를 잘 잡는 앞니가 뻐드러진 나와 동갑이었다

울파주 밖에는 장꾼들을 따라와서 엄지의 젖을 빠는 망아지도 있었다

59

Lonesome Landscape

The young wife who'd been craving sour apricots,[1] on a snowy morning
Her first son came forth

In the deep mountains distant from humanity's cradle
Barked the magpie in the pear tree's thicket

Alone in the darken'd kitchen her father-in-law stands, aged and widowed boiling seaweed soup[2]
And in another dwelling of the village, that same birth soup is boiled[3]

1   Sour apricots (신살구) are often given to expectant mothers for the vitamin C they need.

2   Making seaweed soup, mi-yeok-gug (미역국), for a new mother is traditionally prepared to restore her strength in her first days of taking care of her baby.

3   Birth soup (산국) is an equivalent to seaweed soup.

적경

신살구를 잘도 먹드니 눈오는 아침
나어린 아내는 첫아들을 낳았다

인가 멀은 산 중에
까치는 배나무에서 즞는다

컴컴한 부엌에서는 늙은 홀아비의 시아부지가 미역국을 끓인다
그 마을의 외따른 집에서도 산국을 끓인다

Before Sunrise

With the incessant rooster's call, the Loach Soup Restaurant[1] must
be simmering hangover soup
The kitchen seems warm with the faint light of the fire

With a dim silk covered lantern, as the water man made for the well
Between the stars he stared at the waning moon as tears welled in
his eyes

On the roadway, having dropped in at the early market, the
merchants' paper lamps lit up a donkey's eyes
From inside somewhere, a mournful beating woodblock sounds

1   A restraunt named ChuTang (추탕(鰍湯)) serves dried pond loach soup. The pond
    loach, or mi-ggu-ra-ji (미꾸라지), is a freshwater mudfish.

미명계 (未明界)

자즌닭이 울어서 술국을 끓이는 듯한 추탕(鰍湯)집의
부엌은 뜨수할 것같이 불이 뿌연히 밝다

초롱이 히근하니 물지게꾼이 우물로 가며
별 사이에 바라보는 그믐달은 눈물이 어리었다

행길에는 선장 대여가는 장꾼들의 종이등(燈)에 나귀 눈이 빛났다
어데서 서러웁게 목탁(木鐸)을 뚜드리는 집이 있다

Beside the Castle Gate

On the darkening street outside the castle gate
A man drives forth his swine

No taffy displayed in front of the taffy shop

At road's end a fellow turned his cart with clanging cans
Away to Gangwondo[1]

Upon the tapestry of a tavern's shade, a gaunt shadow rose to knot
her hair[2]

1   Gangwondo (강원도) is a mountainous, forested province in northeast South Korea.
    The man is presumably going there to raise sustenance crops on the mountainside.
2   The act of knotting her hair (머리를 얹혔다) implies in preparation to sell her body.

성외

어두어오는 성문 밖의 거리
도야지를 몰고 가는 사람이 있다

엿방 앞에 엿궤가 없다

양철통을 쩔렁거리며 달구지는 거리 끝에서 강원도로 간다는 길로 든다

술집 문창에 그느슥한 그림자는 머리를 얹혔다

Mountain Morning Autumn Dawning

Amid the morning sunshine, dewdrop marbles on honeysuckle
leisurely ripen, in the valley a pheasant cries to play with the mountain
echo

People atop the mountain ridge, perhaps lumberjacks
As if to fall to the blue sky
The sound of laughter sometimes rolls down the mountain

The monk on a pilgrimage ascends the mountain
Last night in the mountain temple a service was held to pray for the
dead

A cluster of stones slides maybe from the monk's misplaced heel

추일산조 (秋日山朝)

아츰볕에 섶구슬이 한가로이 익은 골짝에서 꿩은 울어 산(山)울림과 장난을
한다

산(山)마루를 탄 사람들은 새꾼들인가
파아란 한울에 떨어질 것같이
웃음소리가 더러 산(山) 밑까지 들린다

순례(巡禮) 중이 산(山)을 올라간다
어젯밤은 이 산(山)절에 재(齋)가 들었다

무리돌이 굴러나리는 건 중의 발굼치에선가

Wide Plain[1]

Raising dust flowers in early spring along a wide plain
The light rail with a mule's heart passes

The ocean appears in the distance
With nothing even resembling a station on the vast plain
The car breaks
A pair of young ladies detrains

1 Gwangwon (광원(曠原)) is the name of an area in Baek Seok's home region of
   Pyeongan Bukdo.

광원 (曠原)

흙꽃 이는 이른 봄의 무연한 벌을
경편철도(輕便鐵道)가 노새의 맘을 먹고 지나간다

멀리 바다가 뵈이는
가정거장(假停車場)도 없는 벌판에서
차(車)는 머물고
젊은 새악시 둘이 나린다

White Night

The moon, over the ancient fortress arose
Atop the thatched roof, a gourd
Like another moon shone brightly
One day in the village, a chaste widow wrapped her neck in a night
of death, yet another night like this

흰밤

옛성(城)의 돌담에 달이 올랐다
묵은 초가지붕에 박이
또 하나 달같이 하이얗게 빛난다
언젠가 마을에서 수절과부 하나가 목을 매여 죽은 밤도 이러한 밤이었다

The Roe
노루

Green Persimmon

On a night of countless stars
To the cool current of a north wind
The persimmon fell green to a dog's harsh bark

청시 (青柿)

별 많은 밤
하누바람이 불어서
푸른 감이 떨어진다 개가 줖는다

Mountain Rain

The raindrops pelt the mulberry leaves

A mountain dove soars

An inchworm atop a stump arches its neck to discern the dove's direction

산비

산(山) 뽕잎에 빗방울이 친다
멧비둘기가 난다
나무등걸에서 자벌기가 고개를 들었다 멧비둘기 켠을 본다

Lonesome Road

A straw mat bundle[1] ascends the side slope at the mountain's back
Ahhh – not another soul on the deserted lonesome road
The mountain crow alone cries and soars
Is it a dispossessed dog that trails aimlessly after
Whether the ground is strewn with fallen cherries, or wild grapes
The thistle and pussy willow's white destiny embraces its eternal
sadness
On a cloudy day like the water in which rice has been washed a spring
wind flutters[2]

1 Changsa (장사) here, refers to a funeral procession and the contents wrapped within the
straw mat a lifeless person bundled up.
2 Dang-pung (동풍(東風)) literally East wind.

78

쓸쓸한 길

거적장사 하나 산(山)뒷 옆비탈을 오른다
아 - 따르는 사람도 없이 쓸쓸한 쓸쓸한 길이다
산(山) 가마귀만 울며 날고
도적갠가 개 하나 어정어정 떠러간다
이스라치전이 드나 머루전이 드나
수리취 땅버들의 하이얀 복이 서러웁다
뚜물같이 흐린 날 동풍(東風)이 설렌다

The Petrified Pomegranate Tree

Its origin the sunny edge of the southern land where the grass never
rises
Living on the cease of rain beams within evening's sunset

From antiquity's beginning
It dreams a mountain hermit of the Tao[1]
To come with herbs picked of the high mountain's fertile soil

Moonbeams of another hometown,
Together with the snow, unite in white to battle the spirit within

---

1   Seon-in-do (선인도) could also be construed as an ascetic, unworldly wizard.

자류

남방토 풀 안 돋은 양지귀가 본이다
햇비 멎은 저녁의 노을 먹고 산다

태고에 나서
선인도가 꿈이다
고산정토에 산약 캐다 오다

달빛은 이향
눈은 정기 속에 어우러진 싸움

Wild Grape Night

The inner room, the light extinguished, the hung white clothes seem
distant like cold coming

In the dog's direction,[1] the sound of a horse bell draws near

Opening the door, in the wild grape light of the night sky
The smell of pine mushrooms wafts

1   A dog's direction (개 방위(方位)로) suggests west-northwest.

머루밤

불을 끈 방안에 횃대의 하이얀 옷이 멀리 추울 것같이

개 방위(方位)로 말방울 소리가 들려온다

문을 연다 머루빛 밤한울에
송이버섯의 내음새가 났다

Buddhist Nun

The Buddhist nun placed her palms together and bowed
The scent of gajichui[1]
A forlorn face, aged as if of a long past
I became mournful as a Buddhist sutra

In P'yongan province, near some deep mountain gold mine, a
market place
    I, of a slight pallid madam, had purchased sweet corn
    The woman, spanking her young daughter, had coolly cried like an
Autumn night

Her estranged husband like a brushwood bee, ten years passed with
her waiting
    The husband unreturned
    The young one, for love of Chinese balloon flowers,[2] to a stone
grave has gone

Even a mountain pheasant dolefully cried, 'twas such a day of
sadness
    Amidst a mountain temple at the garden's edge, the matron's hair
with teardrops fell, 'twas such a day

---

1   Gajichui (가지취) is an edible herb common in Buddhist vegetarian food.
2   Chinese balloon flowers (도라지꽃) often bloom near graves.

여승 (女僧)

여승(女僧)은 합장(合掌)하고 절을 했다
가지취의 내음새가 났다
쓸쓸한 낯이 옛날같이 늙었다
나는 불경(佛經)처럼 서러워졌다

평안도(平安道)의 어느 산 깊은 금덤판
나는 파리한 여인에게서 옥수수를 샀다
여인(女人)은 나어린 딸아이를 따리며 가을밤같이 차게 울었다

섶벌같이 나아간 지아비 기다려 십년(十年)이 갔다
지아비는 돌아오지 않고
어린 딸은 도라지꽃이 좋아 돌무덤으로 갔다

산(山) 꿩도 섧게 울은 슬픈 날이 있었다
산(山) 절의 마당귀에 여인의 머리오리가 눈물방울과 같이 떨어진 날이
있었다

Sura[1]

A little spider descended to the floor, without a thought, I swept it out the door
A cold dark night

Again, in the place where I'd swept the little spider away, a big spider came
My heart stung
As I again sweep the big spider out the door,
Even to the cold outdoors, go to the place your baby went, I lament

In doing so, even before my heartache abated
From somewhere fresh from an infinitesimal egg, a lone leg as yet unformed, emerged an insignificant spider this time coming to the place where the big spider was lost, came in and out of sight
I got all choked up
I say ascend as I offer my hand, but this small thing will undoubtedly sob in fear of me and as it scurries away I mourn this little thing.
I gently place a soft paper to collect and release it outside to be with his mom and sister or brother to worry about this and afterwards if they meet easily it will be good and I grieve.

---

1 Sura (수라 (修羅)) is to become like the Buddhist Asura, a demon forever fighting.

수라 (修羅)

거미새끼 하나 방바닥에 나린 것을 나는 아무 생각 없이 문밖으로
쓸어버린다
　차디찬 밤이다

언제인가 새끼거미 쓸려나간 곳에 큰거미가 왔다
나는 가슴이 짜릿한다
나는 또 큰거미를 쓸어 문밖으로 버리며
찬 밖이라도 새끼 있는 데로 가라고 하며 서러워한다

이렇게 해서 아린 가슴이 싹기도 전이다
어데서 좁쌀알만한 알에서 가제 깨인 듯한 발이 채 서지도 못한 무척 작은
새끼거미가 이번엔 큰거미 없어진 곳으로 와서 아물거린다
　나는 가슴이 메이는 듯하다
　내 손에 오르기라도 하라고 나는 손을 내어미나 분명히 울고불고 할 이
작은 것은 나를 무서우이 달아나버리며 나를 서럽게 한다
　나는 이 작은 것을 고히 보드러운 종이에 받어 또 문밖으로 버리며 이것의
엄마와 누나나 형이 가까이 이것의 걱정을 하며 있다가 쉬이 만나기나 했으면
좋으련만 하고 슬퍼한다

Rain

When did the acacia trees spread their round mat of white petals
Where everywhere the reek of fallen rain extends

비

아카시아들이 언제 흰 두레방석을 깔았나
어데서 물쿤 개비린내가 온다

Roe

Deep in the valley, pounding the earth, we leveled the cottage site, then

On venison, we feasted under a full moon

노루

산(山)골에서는 집터를 츠고 달궤를 닦고
보름달 아래서 노루고기를 먹었다

Beyond the Local Guardian Spirit Totem
국수당 넘어

Tale of a Temple Cow

If sickness comes, the cow going out to the field plucking grass, more than a man in spirit, knows of an herb to heal itself within ten steps

In an old temple of Suyang mountain, an experienced woman past seventy told such a tale as she gathered up edible greens in the pleat of her skirt

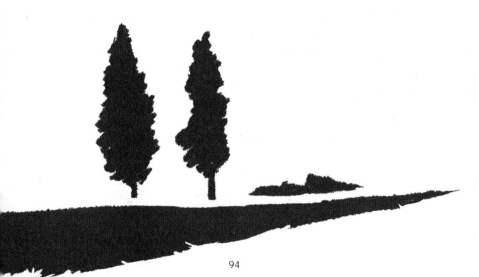

절간의 소 이야기

병이 들면 풀밭으로 가서 풀을 뜯는 소는 인간(人間)보다 영(靈)해서 열 걸음
안에 제 병을 낳게 할 약(藥)이 있는 줄을 안다고

수양산(首陽山)의 어느 오래된 절에서 칠십이 넘은 노장은 이런 이야기를
하며 치마자락의 산나물을 추었다

Tongyeong

Long past, it is said there was a commander of naval forces of this old port, its maidens of length were and yet still many are called 'Chonhee'[1]

Growing gaunt like a strip of seaweed, as an oyster shell emptied, without a word of love, dies

One such Chonhee, amid the fish bones on the wood-floored parlor of a peddler's inn, I encountered

In the dusk of June's end when even the clam at evening cries at the seashore, a seaweed scented rain falls as the dim red glow of the conch lamp scatters across the court

1 · Chonhee (천희 (千姬)) literally "thousand women," is KyoungsangDo dialect for an unmarried woman or maiden with the connotation of a woman of devoted love.

통영 (通營)

옛날엔 통제사(統制使)가 있었다는 낡은 항구(港口)의 처녀들에겐 옛날이
가지 않은 천희(千姬)라는 이름이 많다
　미역오리같이 말라서 굴껍지처럼 말없이 사랑하다 죽는다는
　이 천희(千姬)의 하나를 나는 어느 오랜 객주집의 생선 가시가 있는
마루방에서 만났다
　저문 유월(六月)의 바닷가에선 조개도 울을 저녁 소라방등이
　붉으레한 마당에 김냄새 나는 비가 나렸다

The Place Called Ogeumdeong

At dusk, beside the local guardian spirit shrine's stone wall hanging
from a sumu tree branch, beneath the image of the ghosts of a plague[1]
the young maidens placed rice and greens making incantations
— eat well and go, coil, coil and withdraw, your desire thus fulfilled,
invade us no more

If from the old swamp covered in moss all red, the sound of a brass
lid clanging emerges, someone, eyes swollen with sickness, is calling to
clinging leeches
In the village, on a bruised eye, a sore arm or leg, leeches are
attached

On a night of fox yowls
The sleepless elderly rise to make the sound of spreading beans to
dry[2]
The fox's muzzle points on and howls at a house, the next day
undoubtedly is filled with calamity, what fearful words

---

1 The bodies of those who died of a plague, or nyeo-gui (녀귀), were often burned and
   were therefore not afforded traditional burial rites and spiritual worship.
2 Spreading beans (팥을 깔이며 방뇨를 한다) such a sound is said to be like urination.

오금덩이라는 곳

어스름저녁 국수당 돌각담의 수무나무 가지에 녀귀의 탱을 걸고 나물매
갖추어놓고 비난수를 하는 젊은 새악시들
— 잘 먹고 가라 서리서리 물러가라 네 소원 풀었으니 다시 침노 말아라

벌개늪녘에서 바리깨를 뚜드리는 쇳소리가 나면 누가 눈을 앓어서 부증이
나서 찰거마리를 부르는 것이다
마을에서는 피성한 눈슭에 저린 팔다리에 거마리를 붙인다

여우가 우는 밤이면
잠 없는 노친네들은 일어나 팥을 깔이며 방뇨를 한다
여우가 주둥이를 향하고 우는 집에서는 다음날 으레히 흥사가 있다는 것은
얼마나 무서운 말인가

The Sea at Shiki Harbor[1]

As the rain came at supper
By the sea the boats and men thrived

On the bamboo spear, impaled fish bluer than the sea, from the
house whose stone step was pasted with shellfish came the sound of
entrails falling

Late into the night, on the damp sodden sedge mat moist, the
heartsick man receiving his supper table, unable to eat his tuna was
consumed with tears

On the dark shore's path the pallid face of a maid as if an early
morning moon
Ah, but it's early evening, the sick man closed the seaweed rank door
and, bug like, laid down

1 Located in Shimoda, Shizuoka Prefecture, Japan, Shiki (시기) is the Korean
   pronunciation of the characters 柿崎 which would be pronounced Kakisaki in Japanese.

시기(柿崎)의 바다

저녁밥때 비가 들어서
바다엔 배와 사람이 흥성하다

참대창에 바다보다 푸른 고기가 께우며 섬돌에 곱조개가 붙는 집의
복도에서는 배창에 고기 떨어지는소리가 들렸다

이슥하니 물기에 누굿이 젖은 왕구새자리에서 저녁상을 받은 가슴앓는
사람은 참치회를 먹지 못하고 눈물겨웠다

어득한 기슭의 행길에 얼굴이 해쓱한 처녀가 새벽달같이
아 아즈내인데 병인(炳人)은 미역 냄새 나는 덧문을닫고 버러지같이 누웠다

Jungju Fortress

On a mountain ledge, the melon field lookout stands empty, a lonely
firelight
In the wick of cloth, I seem to hear the pecking of the caster oil

A dragonfly drowses in the crumbling fortress
The fireflies like blue souls all aflutter
From somewhere, as if startled by some soul's utterance, a great
mountain bird to the shadowed valley sails

The ruined remains of the castle gate
As if of a heavenly light, dimly dawns
If day breaks, again a catfish whiskered old man will come to sell
blue pears

정주성 (定州城)

산텃 원두막은 비었나 불빛이 외롭다
헝겊 심지에 아주까리 기름의 쪼는 소리가 들리는 듯하다

잠자리 조을든 무너진 성(城)터
반딧불이 난다 파란 혼(魂)들 같다
어데서 말 있는 듯이 크다란 산(山)새 한 마리 어두운 골짜기로 난다

헐리다 남은 성문(城門)이
한울빛같이 훤하다
날이 밝으면 또 메기수염의 늙은이가 청배를 팔러 올 것이다

Outside ChangEui Gate[1]

In a radish field, a white butterfly flutters near the house where as if from inside its wild grape vine wrapped chestnut tree only the sound of winnowing can be heard

From well's edge, a magpie barks incessantly and then

A red rooster scuttles high on the lumber stack

Near the vegetable plot, the native crab apple tree[2] now with soybean sized bluish eggs hanging down and one-or-two tinged white flowers

By the stone wall, a glossy glazed vessel, a great vase reflects rays of light

---

1 In the ChangEui (창의) area of Chongno, Seoul, the founder of the Chosun dynasty raised four small gates to the city and of those only this one remained.

2 Western apple trees had recently been imported to Korea and Baek Seok chooses this local breed (임금(林檎) 낡) for comparative effect.

창의문외 (彰義門外)

무이밭에 흰나비 나는 집 밤나무 머루넝쿨 속에 키질하는 소리만이 들린다
우물가에서 까치가 자꾸 짖거니 하면
붉은 수탉이 높이 샛더미 위로 올랐다
텃밭가 재래종으 임금(林檎) 낢에는 이제는 콩알 만한 푸른 알이 달렸고
히스무레한 꽃도 하나둘 피여 있다
돌담 기슭에 오지항아리 독이 빛난다

Memorial Gate Village

Painted scarlet there was an old faded memorial gate at the village
edge

'Hyo Ja No Jok Ji Ji Jong Moon'[1] – dust had gathered heaped resting
on the wood carving's quantity
   I, even after ten years of age at the two Ji[2] characters (之之) laughed

Filled with acacia flower's fragrance, a morning of many honeybees
aflight
   Without a ghost, the scops owl having struck the wall's surface with
sharpened beak had perished

Amid the roof tiles, some snake looking bluish in the moonlit night
The children weasel like went around on distant ways

The house of that gate's honor the poor Ganan at fifteen[3]
To an old packhorse driver was wed

---

1   Literally "The Filial Piety of No JokJi's Memorial Gate" ('효자노적지지정문(孝子盧
    迪之之旌門)') or more clearly the Memorial Gate honoring the Filial Piety of the good
    son, No JokJi.

2   Normally Ji (之) means 'to go' or 'of' but the repeated jiji (지지) is what a parent would
    say to a young child so they don't touch something dirty.

3   Ganan (가난), a girl's name meaning 'new-born', also carries the connotation of the
    Korean word for 'poor'.

정문촌 (旌門村)

주홍칠이 날은 정문(旌門)이 하나 마을 어구에 있었다

'효자노적지지정문(孝子盧迪之之旌門)' – 몬지가 겹겹이 앉은 목각(木刻)의 액(額)에
나는 열 살이 넘도록 갈지자(字) 둘을 웃었다

아카시아꽃의 향기가 가득하니 꿀벌들이 많이 날어드는 아츰
구신은 없고 부헝이가 담벽을 띠쫗고 죽었다

기왓골에 배암이 푸르스름히 빛난 달밤이 있었다
아이들은 쪽재피같이 먼길을 돌았다

정문집 가난이는 열다섯에
늙은 말꾼한테 시집을 갔겄다

Fox Valley

A gourd boiling inside the house
Grandfather and grandson scale the rooftop, the sky a glaring green
The well water below must merely be bitter

In the village, the day for steaming hemp to strip
A rumor of a drowning from the following village came

On a thick blanket of yellow bush clover leaves arranged under the
awning, I laid out a recently woven arrowroot mat, sat and savored the
pumpkin rice cakes

A mimicking mountain jaybird eating a wild pear in the valley,
eating the issue of wild pear trees begets an aching belly that the
children say heals by eating unripe pears

여우난골

박을 삶는 집
할아버지와 손자가 오른 지붕 위에 한울빛이 진초록이다
우물의 물이 쓸 것만 같다

마을에서는 삼굿을 하는 날
건넌마을서 사람이 물에 빠져 죽었다는 소문이 왔다

노란 싸리잎이 한불 깔린 토방에 햇칡방석을 깔고 나는 호박떡을 맛있게도
먹었다

어치라는 산새는 벌배 먹어 고흡다는 골에서 돌배 먹고 아픈 배를
아이들은 떨배를 먹고 나었다고 하였다

Sambang[1]

Like a woven trinket of reeds, the fresh mountain spring road
twisted, replete with wooden bowls and arguta vine walking sticks

From fifteen li[2] over the mountain, hoisting vessels hollowed from
tree's trunks and wearing bush clover slippers damp, doused with
mountain rain, even the backwoods brood came to fetch mineral
water

In a lower village, adolescent shamans often occasion to stand on a
straw chopper's cruel edge to perform a spirit exorcism

---

1 Sambang (삼방(三防)) was a village in Hamgyong Namdo famous for its mineral springs.
The poem was originally entitled Sanji (산지) meaning Mountain Village.

2 15-li (리) is about 7.5 km or 5 miles.

삼방 (三防)

갈부던 같은 약수(藥水)터의 산(山)거리엔 나무그릇과 다래나무지팽이가 많다

산(山) 너머 십오리(十五里)서 나무뒝치 차고 싸리신 신고 산(山)비에 촉촉이 젖어서 약(藥)물을 받으려 오는 두멧아이들도 있다

아랫마을에서는 애기무당이 작두를 타며 굿을 하는 때가 많다

Series Poems 연작시

The Road to Changwon[1]
Poem of a trip to the South 1

Hidden behind the small pine tree
Hoping to surprise the hare or pheasant, a hillside road

Feeling like laying flat to warm my hands on this road

With a dog, ho-ee ho-ee whistling[2]
Feeling like going on with worries left behind on this road

Taking off my bundle, building a fire and sitting
Feeling like smoking a single cigarette on this road

Coyotes in row upon row hanging back in tow as I go
Wishing for friendly banter on this road

A pony-tailed bachelor, shouldering his beloved hoping to come on
this road

---

1 Changwon (창원) is the capital city of Gyeongsangnam-do, on the southeast coast.
2 Ho-ee ho-ee (호이호이) onomatopoeia for a whistle.

창원도 (昌原道)
남행시초 (南行詩抄) 1

솔포기에 숨었다
토끼나 꿩을 놀래주고 싶은 산허리의 길은

엎데서 따스하니 손 녹히고 싶은 길이다

개 데리고 호이호이 회파람 불며
시름 놓고 가고 싶은 길이다

궤나리봇짐 벗고 땃불 놓고 앉어
담배 한 대 피우고 싶은 길이다

승냥이 줄레줄레 달고 가며
덕신덕신 이야기하고 싶은 길이다

더꺼머리 총각은 정든 님 업고 오고 싶은 길이다

Tongyeong
Poem of a trip to the South 2

Tongyeong market began a day

One new horsehair hat to wear, a hundred dried persimmons
bought, a length of red silk ribbon cut, and a bottle of some brew in
hand

To sense a steamboat's feel, I stepped on deck

Returning, in front of a guest house as a girl goes in
I listen to a leper sing a Poomba song[1]

As the moon of the seventeenth day rises
Taking a ferry, I cross the canal

---

1 A poomba song (품바타령) is a beggar's song based on a traditional Korean ballad
named Taryeong (타령).

통영 (統營)
남행시초 (南行詩抄) 2

통영(統營)장 낫대들었다

갓 한닢 스고 건시 한접 사고 홍공단 댕기 한감 끊고
술 한병 받어들고

화륜선 만저보려 선창 갔다

오다 가수내 들어가는 주막 앞에
문둥이 품바타령 듣다가

열이레 달이 올라서
나룻배 타고 판데목 지나간다 간다

The Road to GoSeong
Poem of a trip to the South 3

On the road to GoSeong market
The sun buoyant, hovering high

A village of no dogs
In the right sunny courtyard's corner, a round straw mat[1]
Red and yellow
Dazzling and fair, the dried rice
Ah, azaleas and forsythia in full bloom
A feast nearing

Fair flavored rice drying
Such a happy village

Somehow, the young women wearing dark red skirts and yellow
jackets
Might likely live laughing in this village

1 Such mats, or mae-bang-seok (맷방석), are often spread under a millstone

118

고성가도 (固城街道)
남행시초 (南行詩抄) 3

고성(固城)장 가는 길
해는 둥둥 높고

개 하나 얼린하지 않는 마을은
해발은 마당귀에 맷방석 하나
빨갛고 노랗고
눈이 서울은 곱기도 한 건반밥
아 진달래 개나리 한창 피었구나
가까이 잔치가 있어서

곱디고운 건반밥을 말리우는 마을은
얼마나 즐거운 마을인가

어쩐지 당홍치마 노란저고리 입은 새악시들이
웃고 살을 것만 같은 마을이다

SamChon Port
Poem of a trip to the South 4

In row upon row the piglets go

Earlobe numbing prickly rays in plenty, the warming street
Up an ash heap the magpie mounts, the child mounts, the haze
mounts

In the threshing yard good for warming in the sun
People stand around like rice-straw, yellowish
As if on a day of fresh fallen snow after clearing it away, an argument
rang out yellow

A packsaddle cow dozes

Ah, everything warm and poor

삼천포 (三千浦)
남행시초 (南行詩抄) 4

졸레졸레 도야지새끼들이 간다
귀밑이 재릿재릿하니 볕이 담복 따사로운 거리다

잿더미에 까치 오르고 아이 오르고 아지랑이 오르고

해바라기하기 좋을 볏곡간 마당에
볏짚같이 누우런 사람들이 둘러서서
어느 눈 오신 날 눈을 치고 생긴 듯한 말다툼 소리도 3 누우러니

소는 기르매 지고 조은다

아 모도들 따사로히 가난하니

Bukguan[1]
Poems of a trip to Hamju 1

With salted guts of a walleye pollack with red pepper paste and
radish makings abruptly minced and mixed this seasoned thing
This unshapely rough Bukguan as I sit and endlessly examine to feel
Lonely with knees as if cut off

Inside that sourish, fishy, fetid and foul smell
I faintly sense the smell of the flesh of Yojin[2]

Within this pungent peppery, fishy foul stinking taste
I also discern the far off peasants of Shilla's nostalgic scent[3]

1 Bukguan (북관(北關)) is a region of northern Korea.

2 Yojin (여진(女眞)) is a family or tribe of Manchuria that formed the Ching Dynasty in China.

3 Shilla (신라(新羅)) is the dynasty that outlasted the three kingdoms period and developed much of Korea's culture.

북관 (北關)
함주시초 (咸州詩抄) 1

명태(明太) 창난젓에 고추무거리에 막칼질한 무이를
비벼 익힌 것을
이 투박한 북관(北關)을 한없이 끼밀고 있노라면
쓸쓸하니 무릎은 끊어진다

시큼한 배척한 퀴퀴한 이 내음새 속에
나는 가느슥히 여진(女眞)의 살내음새를 맡는다

얼큰한 비릿한 구릿한 이 맛 속에선
까마득히 신라(新羅) 백성의 향수(鄕愁)도 맛본다

A Roe
Poems of a trip to Hamju 2

The land of Jangjin county just a neck-stretch over the roof
With something like a Silk tree
Sweet millet drink[1] and millet tea rice cakes everywhere and
On this street some deep mountain peasant led a fawn
The mountain peasant wearing a rough hemp overcoat and rough
hemp breeches
    In imitation of the fawn
    Stroking the fawn's back
    Claiming that before a vacant lot it ate all the kidney bean sprouts
and
    Calling for a price of thirdy-fi nyang[2]
The fawn's fur sparsely spotted with white and it's belly billowed
with shedding fluff
    In imitation of the mountain peasant

    Licking the mountain peasant's hand
As if understanding the haggling over medicinal qualities[3]
In black eyes something white almost overflowing

---

1 A Sweet millet drink (기장감주) is a sweet fermented drink similar to Shikae, but made from millet.

2 35 nyang (냥) in the Yi dynasty the unit of money was a nyang and the thirdy-fi (서른 닷냥) is 35 pronounced with the local dialect.

3 A fawn's musk gland near the belly button is used in traditional medicines (약자).

노루
함주시초 (咸州詩抄) 2

장진(長津) 땅이 지붕넘어 넘석하는 거리다
자구나무 같은 것도 있다
기장감주에 기장차떡이 흔한데다
이 거리에 산골사람이 노루새끼를 다리고 왔다
산골사람은 막베 등거리 막베 잠방등에를 입고
노루새끼를 닮었다
노루새끼 등을 쓸며
터 앞에 당콩순을 다 먹었다 하고
서른닷냥 값을 부른다
노루새끼는 다문다문[1] 흰 점이 백이고 배안의 털을 너슬너슬 벗고[2]
산골사람을 닮었다

산골사람의 손을 핥으며
약자에 쓴다는 흥정소리를 듣는 듯이
새까만 눈에 하이얀 것이 가랑가랑하다

1 Damun damun (다문다문) is dialect for deumun deumun
   (드문드문) meaning sparsely or thinly scattered.

2 Neoseul neoseul (너슬너슬) is dialect for
   neoul-neoul (너울너울) an onomatopoeic
   word meaning waveringly or swaying or billowing.

Ancient Temple
Poems of a trip to Hamju 3

The budumak,[1] the height of two men[2]
At this budumak a ladder placed, the wispy bearded monk who
prepares rice
Ascended carrying Buddha's rice

Cooking one mal of rice,[3] the great-grand rice pot
Turning away and sitting cross-legged entitled to count beads

With many-bundled cluster of branch they say this furnace
Even this grim sinister furnace fears Choangnim[4]

The wooden floor and the paper wind wall all in veiled thought
Think of white rice and tofu and fried kelp and salted fish

With an earned yawn, the devotion bowl and the brass bowl
Quietly cross-armed and squatting

With no one praying for some soul's departure, with no fire in this
dark and lightless land
If Choangnim tells a scary story
Everyone as dead would lay face down and be consumed with sleep

---

1   A cooking fireplace or budumak (부뚜막) is a traditional earthen platform in which an iron pot for cooking rice is embedded and under which the fire is tended.

2   Here two kil (두 길) could also equal 20 cha (1 cha = 30.3cm).

3   One mal (말) is about eight kilograms, generally used as a measurement of rice or grain.

4   Choangnim (조앙님은) is the name of a kitchen god.

고사 (古寺)
함주시초 (咸州詩抄) 3

부뚜막이 두 길이다
이 부뚜막에 놓인 사닥다리로 자박수염난 공양주는
성궁미를 지고 오른다

한말 밥을 한다는 크나큰 솥이
외면하고 가부틀고 앉아서 염주도 세일 만하다

화라지송침이 단채로 들어간다는 아궁지
이 험상궂은 아궁지도 조앙님은 무서운가보다

농마루며 바람벽은 모두들 그느슥히
흰밥과 두부와 튀각과 자반을 생각나 하고

하펌도 남즉하니 불기와 유종들이
묵묵히 팔장끼고 쭈구리고 앉었다

재 안 드는 밤은 불도 없이 캄캄한 까막나라에서
조앙님은 무서운 이야기나 하면
모두들 죽은 듯이 엎데었다 잠이 들 것이다

A Note to Friends at Dinner
Poems of a trip to Hamju 4

On the old tray, white rice and crawfish and I come out to sit
And welcome the taste of a lonely dinner

White rice and crawfish and me
Together we would talk about anything
Together in trust and intimacy and, ah we feel good

Since we, beneath the clear water on the sandy bank of the estuary's
long, long day,
Count grains of sand one by one, our bones growing old

Since we, in the grand field where the wind is good listening to the
sheldrake sound got older drinking sweet dew

Since we, in the solitary mountain valley studying the sound of a
hawk and befriending a chipmunk growing up

We all were bleached white without greed
Kind and sweet, without a thorny spirit, without a heavy hand
This pale form being much too neat and proper

Even in poverty, we are not sad
Without reason to be lonesome
And never envious of anyone

White rice and crawfish and me
We, as we are
It seems, should leave something like the world behind

선우사 (膳友辭)
함주시초 (咸州詩抄) 4

낡은 나조반에 흰밥도 가재미도 나도 나와 앉어서
쓸쓸한 저녁을 맞는다

흰 밥과 가재미와 나는
우리들은 그 무슨 이야기라도 다 할 것 같다
우리들은 서로 미덥고 정답고 그리고 서로 좋구나

우리들은 맑은 물 밑 해정한 모래톱에서 하구 긴 날을
모래알만 헤이며 잔뼈가 굵은 탓이다

바람 좋은 한벌판에서 물닭이 소리를 들으며 단이슬
먹고 나이들은 탓이다

외따른 산골에서 소리개소리 배우며 다람쥐 동무하고
자라난 탓이다.

우리들은 모두 욕심이 없어 희여졌다
착하디 착해서 세괏은 가시 하나 손아귀 하나 없다
너무나 정갈해서 이렇게 파리했다

우리들은 가난해도 서럽지 않다
우리들은 외로워할 까닭도 없다
그리고 누구 하나 부럽지도 않다

흰밥과 가재미와 나는
우리들이 같이 있으면
세상 같은 건 밖에 나도 좋을 것 같다

Mountain Valley
Poems of a trip to Hamju 5

On a stone wall, a cluster of wild grapes ripens black
In a gravelly field, caster beans spill out
A sunny valley with a soft rustling breeze
I sought a house in this valley to last the winter
A valley of few houses
Every garden laid out with ingredients for winter kimchi
And in the yard gathered stalks in stacks
Realizing the passage of time an empty seeming house unseen
I passed deeper and deeper into the valley

At valley's end bellow the mountain's foot, one smallish stone
roofed house stood
This house's mistress with blue-trimmed top had said when winter
comes she'd let me the house and go down the road around the
mountain
In the sunny yard were kept more than twenty hives of bees

As the day grew long the sun's rays tickling the porches edge I sat
with hanging feet
The last summer taking a truck down to the land of Jangjin harbor
to collect honey and coming back
Looking on these bees I imagine
The days soon growing cold and wild chrysanthemums withering
The diligent people all in their homes
I ponder coming to this valley

산곡 (山谷)
함주시초 (咸州詩抄) 5

돌각담에 머루송이 깜하니 익고
자갈밭에 아즈까리 알이 쏟아지는
잠풍하니 볕바른 골짜기이다
나는 이 골짝에서 한겨울을 날려고 집을 한채 구하였다
집이 몇 집 되지 않는 골안은
모두 터알에 김장감이 퍼지고
뜨락에 잡곡 낟가리가 쌓여서
어니 세월에 비일 듯한 집은 뵈이지 않았다
나는 자꾸 골안으로 깊이 들어갔다

골이 다한 산대 밑에 자그마한 돌능와집이 한채 있어서
이집 남길동 단 안주인은 겨울이면 집을 내고
산을 돌아 거리로 나려간다는 말을 하는데
해바른 마당에는 꿀벌이 스무나문 통 있었다

낮 기울은 날을 햇볕 장글장글한 툇마루에 걸어앉어서
지난 여름 도락구를 타고 장진(長津)땅에 가서 꿀을
치고 돌아왔다는 이 벌들을 바라보며 나는
날이 어서 추워져서 숙국화꽃도 시들고
이 바즈런한 백성들도 다 제 집으로 들은 뒤에
이 골안으로 올 것을 생각하였다

Mountain Lodge
Deep Mountain Chants 1

Call it a lodging house but a noodle house it will be

Heaped with full up burlap bags of buckwheat flour, the upper room
in fact rarely feels the heat

I laid along the old noodle apparatus

As I tried to rest my head on the rolly, roundish wooden pillows
tossed in the corner

I ponder the people visiting that mountain village whose sweat had
stained those blocks black with their being

I try to imagine their faces and feelings and life's work

산숙 (山宿)
산중음 (山中吟) 1

여인숙이라도 국수집이다

메밀가루포대가 그득하니 쌓인 웃간을 들믄들믄 더웁기도 하다

나는 낡은 국수분틀과 그즈런히 나가 누어서

구석에 데굴데굴하는 목침(木枕)들을 베여보며

이 산(山)골에 들어와서 이 목침들에 새까마니 때를 올리고 간 사람들을

생각한다

그 사람들의 얼굴과 생업(生業)과 마음들을 생각해 본다

The Sound of Sacred Rites
Deep Mountain Chants 2

The crescent moon as if a spirit fire on this fearful mountain valley way

At the eaves edge the paper lamp burns bright

Jjeorag-jjeorag striking the rice cakes[1]

They're potato rice cakes

Now only this dark-dark night and the sound of a running brook remain

1   Jjeorag-jjeorag (쩌락 쩌락) onomatopoeia for the sound of a mallet striking dough.

향악 (鄕樂)
산중음 (山中吟) 2

초생달이 귀신불같이 무서운 산(山)골거리에선
처마 끝에 종이등이 불을 밝히고
쩌락쩌락 떡을 친다
감자떡이다
이젠 캄캄한 밤과 개울물 소리만이다

Deep Night
Deep Mountain Chants 3

In the earthen-floored room, the coyote-like puppy sits
Within the kitchen plumes of steam rise and swell
Much past midnight
The hen caught, rolling out buckwheat noodles
Near some mountain yap and yelp, a barking fox cries

야반 (夜半)
산중음 (山中吟) 3

토방에 승냥이 같은 강아지가 앉은 집
부엌으론 무럭무럭 하이얀 김이 난다
자정도 활신 지났는데
닭을 잡고 메밀국수를 누른다고 한다
어느 산(山) 옆에선 캥캥 여우가 운다

White Birch
Deep Mountain Chants 4

Even the mountain valley house's cross beams, even pillars even the
door lattice ribs are white birch wood

If at night the barking foxes yap and yelp, even the mountain is
white birch wood

Even the firewood for boiling those delicious buckwheat noodles' is
white birch wood

And like the sweet dew even the gourd serving the pleasing spring
water of the surging shallow source is white birch wood

Past the mountain they say even the land of Pyungando can be seen,
all this mountain valley is white birch wood

백화 (白樺)
산중음 (山中吟) 4

산골집은 대들보도 기둥도 문살도 자작나무다
밤이면 캥캥 여우가 우는 산(山)도 자작나무다
그 맛있는 메밀국수를 삶는 장작도 자작나무다
그리고 감로(甘露)같이 단샘이 솟는 박우물도 자작나무다
산(山) 너머는 평안도(平安道) 땅도 뵈인다는 이 산(山) 골은 온통 자작나무다

Samho
Sheldrake Sound 1[1]

At the foot of its gate the upside-down sea character hung house[2]
Upon the fresh blue reed mat jjiruk jjiruk[3]
Eating the crying shellfish I spend a midsummer

Spending a midsummer so with shellfish
Together accumulating lines in the lazy flow of water
With thickening waist I find myself fondly attached to one person

1 A sheldrake (물닭) is a large, fish-eating, brightly-colored, Old World diving duck with a crested head and a long bill notched like the blade of a saw.

2 A sea character (바다 햇자) refers to a traditional Chinese character meaning "sea."

3 Jjireuk jjireuk (찌륵찌륵) is onomatopoeia for the sound of slurping.

삼호 (三湖)
물닭의 소리 1

문기슭에 바다햇자를 까꾸로 붙인 집
산듯한 청삿자리 위에서 찌륵찌륵
우는 전복회를 먹어 한여름을 보낸다

이렇게 한여름을 보내면서 나는 하늑이는
물살에 나이금이 느는 꽃조개와 함께
허리도리가 굵어가는 한 사람을 연연해 한다

Mulgyeri[1]
Sheldrake Sound 2

Underwater – the fine sand a wooden dipper to wash out small shellfish

A long sandy beach – the sea hung out,[2] unbelieving comes in and out

As if this roll of silk might tear meanly heeled

These warps and wefts all became dulcimer strings jing-jingling

1 Mulgaeri 물계리(物界里) literally "Mundane World Town."

2 Hung out (널어놓고) as if laundry on a line.

물계리 (物界里)
물닭의 소리 2

    물밑 — 이 세모래 닌함박은 콩조개만 일다

    모래장변 — 바다가 널어놓고 못미더워 드나드는 명주필을 짓궂이
발뒤축으로 찢으면

    날과 씨는 모두 양금줄이 되어 짜랑짜랑 울었다

Daesan Dong[1]
Sheldrake Sound 3

Biaegoji biaegoji[2]

These are your words swallow

Over there on Roe Island there are no roes you say

On Shinmi island's Samgak Mountain they raise only dark round

shellfish you say

Biaegoji biaegoji

These are your words swallow

The blue sea the white sky are good and good you say

On the bright sandy beach a stone monument stands you say

Biaegoji biaegoji

These are your words swallow

The red-eyed seagull the red seagull should go away so you say

Howling like a coyote the seagull

Scary go away so you say

---

1   Daesan Dong (대산동(大山洞)) town near Gwangju in the south, literally "Great Mountain."

2   Biaegoji (비애고지) is onomatopoeia for the tweet, trill and twitter, chitter-chattering of swallows. The name also relates to the steep slopes of the village, Bipaburak (비파부락).

대산동 (大山洞)
물닭의 소리 3

비얘고지 비얘고지는
제비야 네 말이다
저 건너 노루섬에 노루 없드란 말이지
신미도 삼각산엔 가무래기만 나드란 말이지

비얘고지 비얘고지는
제비야 네 말이다
푸른 바다 흰 한울이 좋기도 좋단 말이지
해밝은 모래장변에 돌비 하나 섰단 말이지

비얘고지 비얘고지는
제비야 네 말이다
눈빨갱이 갈매기 빨갱이 갈매기 가란 말이지
승냥이처럼 우는 갈매기
무서워 가란 말이지

145

NamHyang[1]
Sheldrake Sound 4

At the blue seashore, the white, white road

Children in row upon row drive green bamboo horses
The hawksbill poongjam[2] wearing old man went with a snipe[3]
hanging

This road
After some distance, a village with sweet dew water gushing
On the white plastered wall, the old-time tray-round clock hung
This house with single mother and her waterfoul-like only daughter
A place with talk of being betrothed spread out in a haze.

1   NamHyang (남향(南鄉)) literally "Southern Town," probably on the South Sea.

2   A small accessory worn on a traditional Korean inner hat, poongjam (풍잠) is weighted
    to hold the outer horsehair hat (갓), onto the head so as not to fly away in the wind.

3   A snipe (또요) is a wading bird with a long slender bill and camouflage plumage.

남향 (南鄕)
물닭의 소리 4

푸른 바닷가의 하이얀 하이얀 길이다

아이들은 늘늘히 청대나무말을 몰고
대모풍잠한 늙은이 또요 한 마리를 드리우고 갔다

이 길이다
얼마 가서 감로(甘露) 같은 물이 솟는 마을 하이얀 회담벽에 옛적본의
쟁반시계를 걸어놓은 집 홀어미와 사는 물새 같은 외딸의 혼삿말이
아지랑이같이 낀 곳은

Sentiments of a Rainy Night
Sheldrake Sound 5

Amid the dark, dark rain
The deep red moon rising
White flowers blooming
From a distant foothold a dog barking night
From somewhere a watery scented night

Amid the dark, dark rain
The deep red moon rising
White flowers blooming
From the distant foothold a dog barks
From somewhere this watery scented night

As if those things familiar to me, the eggplant, pollack, roe deer,
quail, clay jars, yellow butterfly, wild flowers, buckwheat noodles,
blue skirts, and the collection of straw shoes surrounded with pretty
seashells and I endlessly missed the girl called Chonhi tonight

야우소회 (夜雨小懷)
물닭의 소리 5

캄캄한 비 속에
새빨간 달이 뜨고
하이얀 꽃이 퓌고
먼바루 개가 짖는 밤은
어데서 물의 내음새 나는 밤이다

캄캄한 비 속에
새빨간 달이 뜨고
하이얀 꽃이 퓌고
먼바루 개가 짖고
어데서 물의 내음새 나는 밤은

나의 정다운 것들 가지 명태 노루 뫼추리 질동이 노랑나비 바구지꽃
메밀국수 남치마 자개짚세기 그리고 천희(天姫)라는 이름이 한없이
그리워지는 밤이로구나

Ggolddugi[1]

Sheldrake Sound 6

In the net of the new dawn
Entrapped are the ggolddugi of my liking
Gat wearing and kind hearted
Caught in the rice stalk net for what

The seagulls alight

The spurting ink from your mouth
Is it magic made from decades of development
Moving back and forth as you wish
Having read Sun Tzu's book of military science
The seagulls murmur

But now the squid strewn on the pier
Crying as if young birds beside
I sit saddened and listen to the boatmen tell of the day when nine
together shared sliced raw ggolddugi each with a share remaining to
take away

The seagulls take flight

---

1 Ggolddugi (꼴뚜기), correctly spelled 꼴뚜기, or beka squid is tied to luck and fortune.
Additionally, an octopus dealer carries the connotation of a man of broken fortunes and
yet a proverb (장마다 꼴뚜기 나랴) states that one cannot expect ggolddugi at every
market, essentially, "good luck does not always repeat itself."

꼴뚜기
물닭의 소리 6

신새벽 들망에
내가 좋아하는 꼴두기가 들었다
갓 쓰고 사는 마음이 어진데
새끼 그물에 걸리는 건 어인 일인가

갈매기 날어온다

입으로 먹을 뿜는 건
몇 십 년 도를 닦어 피는 조환가
앞뒤로 가기를 마음대로 하는 건
손자(孫子)의 병서(兵書)도 읽은 것이다
갈매가 쭝얼댄다

그러나 시방 꼴두기는 배창에 너불어저 새새기 같은 울음을 우는 곁에서
뱃사람들의 언젠가 아홉이서 회를 처먹고도 남어 한 깃씩 나눠가지고
갔다는 크디큰 꼴두기의 이야기를 들으며 나는 슬프다

갈매기 날어난다

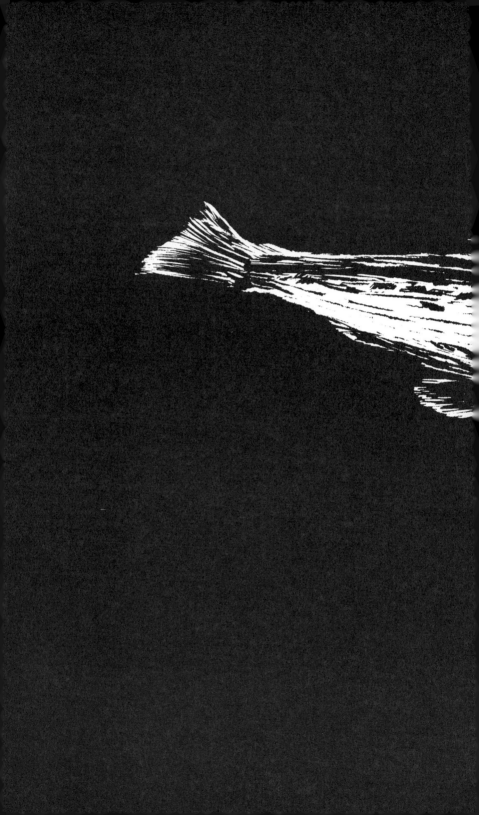

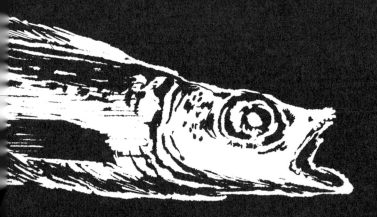

The Heart's Wanderings
종잡을 수 없는 마음

Poems of Place, Passing Beauty & Love's Loss
장소, 시간에 따른 아름다움과 잃어버린 사랑

Tongyeong

On Guma[1] Mountain's wharf she weeps descending from the boat, a
half-day of waves cresting its deck
  Quite close to the town producing horsehair hats

The taste of wind somewhat salty, the taste of sea salty too

Good for fresh abalone, trepang,[2] red snapper and flatfish
Good for pickled sea lettuce, branchia and small octopus too

A drum sounds the street 'kwang kwang' at the break of dawn
A boat sounds the sea 'bbung bbung' all night long

Despite sleep's disruption a place where you desire to rise and set off
for the sea

A place where house by house codfish dry child-sized and with
blood remaining
  A place where an old traveling trader speaks Japanese well
  A place where maidens all wish to marry the fishing banks master

On the road over the mountain a maiden stands by the stone wall
with head hung like the girl called Geum[3]
  The young daughter at Masan Travelers Inn where I stay seems like

---

1 Guma Mountain (구마산(舊馬山)) literally translated is 'Old Horse Mountain.'

2 A trepang (해삼) is a large sea cucumber that lives in the southern Pacific and Indian
   oceans eaten in soups, especially in China and Indonesia. Genera: Holothuria Actinopyga

3 A literal translation of the name Geum (금(錦)) would be 'Silk.'

the girl called Nan[4]

The girl named Nan lives in MyungJung village[5]

The village over the mountain called MyungJung village with rich green camellia trees

And sweet dew water gushing from MyungJung fountain

Amid the noise and bustle of young wedded women drawing water might be that girl of my fancy

That girl of my fancy in the season of green branch with red, red camellia blossoms

Is likely to marry into some distant town's family

A woman wearing long armlets[6] and a wig winding her way up the mountain pass

As if coming from Pyungando in the season of camellias' bloom when will it pass

This night I plop down on the stone step of a worn shrine to some ancient deified commander

As if to cry and cry becoming the boatman in HanSan Island's sea

A low straw thatched house a low fenced house in the house with only the courtyard high carrying fourteen moons on her back with only a mortar to pound I think of my woman[7]

---

4 The name Nan's (난(蘭)) literal translation is 'Orchid.'

5 MyungJung (명정(明井)) literally means 'Bright Fountain.'

6 Wearing long armlets (긴 토시 끼고) suggests cold weather.

7 Here 'my person' (내 사람) implies his wife was left behind in Pyungando.

통영 (統營)

구마산(舊馬山)의 선창에선 좋아하는 사람이 울며 나리는 배에 올라서 오는
물길이 반날
갓 나는 고당은 가깝기도 하다

바람맛도 짭짤한 물맛도 짭짤한

전복에 해삼에 도미 가재미의 생선이 좋고
파래에 아개미에 호루기의 젓갈이 좋고

새벽녘의 거리엔 쾅쾅 북이 울고
밤새껏 바다에선 뿡뿡 배가 울고

자다가도 일어나 바다로 가고 싶은 곳이다

집집이 아이만한 피도 안 간 대구를 말리는 곳
황화장사 영감이 일본말을 잘도 하는 곳
처녀들은 모두 어장주(漁場主) 한테 시집을 가고 싶어한다는 곳

산 너머로 가는 길 돌각담에 갸웃하는 처녀는 금(錦)이라든 이 같고
내가 들은 마산(馬山) 객주(客主)집의 어린 딸은 난(蘭)이라는 이 같고

난(蘭)이라는 이는 명정(明井)골에 산다는데
명정(明井)골은 산을 넘어 동백(冬栢)나무 푸르른 감로(甘露)같은 물이 솟는
명정(明井) 샘이 있는 마을인데
샘터엔 오구작작 물을 긷는 처녀며 새악시들 가운데 내가 좋아하는 그이가
있을 것만 같고
내가 좋아하는 그이는 푸른 가지 붉게붉게 동백꽃 피는 철엔 타관 시집을
갈 것만 같은데

긴 토시 끼고 큰머리 얹고 오불고불 넘엣거리로 가는 여인은
평안도(平安道)서 오신 듯한데 동백(冬栢)꽃 피는 철이 그 언제요

옛 장수 모신 낡은 사당의 돌층계에 주저앉어서 나는 이 저녁
울 듯 울 듯 한산도(閑山島) 바다에 뱃사공이 되어가며
넝 낮은 집 담 낮은 집 마당만 높은 집에서 열나흘 달을 업고
손방아만 찧는 내 사람을 생각한다

The Sea

Despite escaping to the sea's side
The sea it seems comes only with thoughts of you
It seems the sea and I want only for love of you

Ascending the curved body of the sandy plain
You seem to walk before me
And emerge again behind

And letting lapping thoughts wear my walk of water's edge
As if only in your words impression
As if only in your words halt

This side of the sea,
A Morning Glory devoid of morning
With white sunshine on shiny scales glaring cold,
Somehow seeming lonesome, somehow seeming sorrowful

바다

바닷가에 왔드니
바다와 같이 당신이 생각만 나는구려
바다와 같이 당신을 사랑하고만 싶구려

구붓하고 모래톱을 오르면
당신이 앞선 것만 같구려
당신이 뒤선 것만 같구려

그리고 지중지중 물가를 거닐면
당신이 이야기를 하는 것만 같구려
당신이 이야기를 끊는 것만 같구려

바닷가는
개지꽃이 개지 아니 나오고
고기비눌에 하이얀 햇볕만 쇠리쇠리하야
어쩐지 쓸쓸만 하구려 섧기만 하구려

Me, Natasha and the White Donkey

Poor in my poverty
As I loved the beautiful Natasha
Tonight the snow descended completely

I love Natasha
The snow but soft, falls fast
Drinking soju,[1] sitting in loneliness
Drinking soju, and thinking
Of Natasha and I
As the snow builds in the night, we ride the white donkey
Let's go to the valley
To where the tit cries deep in the valley
To live in a cottage, let's go

The weighted snow tumbles
I ponder Natasha
She cannot but come
Already come, calm inside me and to my heart whispered
The valley retreat, 'tis no sign of defeat to this world
Something as such we forsake for all its sullied and soiled foulness

The snow weighted, plummets
The beautiful Natasha loves me and
From somewhere the white donkey will cry with glee for the night
"hee-haw hee-haw"

---

1   Soju (소주) is a clear Korean alcohol made from rice, wheat or barley.

나와 나타샤와 흰 당나귀

가난한 내가
아름다운 나타샤를 사랑해서
오늘밤은 푹푹 눈이 나린다

나타샤를 사랑은 하고
눈은 푹푹 날리고
나는 혼자 쓸쓸히 앉어 소주(燒酒)를 마신다
소주를 마시며 생각한다
나타샤와 나는
눈이 푹푹 쌓이는 밤 흰 당나귀 타고
산골로 가자 출출이 우는 깊은 산골로 가 마가리*에 살자

눈은 푹푹 나리고
나는 나타샤를 생각하고
나타샤가 아니 올 리 없다
언제 벌써 내 속에 고조곤히 와 이야기한다
산골로 가는 것은 세상한테 지는 것이 아니다
세상 같은 건 더러워 버리는 것이다

눈은 푹푹 나리고
아름다운 나타샤는 나를 사랑하고
어데서 흰 당나귀도 오늘밤이 좋아서 응앙응앙 울을 것이다

Iduguk Harbor Highway[1]

The old-time cloth-covered coach

From some village with a new bride riding together

To some coastal avenue they are said to go

Passing village upon village with yellow golden mandarins

Eating young and fresh golden mandarins, how joyful is that

1 Pronounced 'Izuno Kuni Minado Gaido' in Japanese, the Izu (伊豆) Peninsula is in
   Shizuoka Prefecture, Japan and Minado (湊) is a small port located in the southern end
   of the Peninsula. Izu became well-known through Kawabata's celebrated novella "The
   Dancer of Izu."

이두국주가도 (伊豆國湊街道)

옛적본의 휘장마치에
어느메 촌중의 새 새악시와도 함께 타고
먼 바닷가의 거리로 간다는데
금귤이 누런 마을마을을 지나가며
싱싱한 금귤을 먹는 것은 얼마나 즐거운 일인가

Despair

The ladies of Bukwan are robust
The ladies of Bukwan are fair
One especially fair and robust lass
Her white jacket, attached with red
To harmonize with the black skirt of her hanbok,
To think on her was a delightful dream
One morning this lass
A heavy jar above her brow
In her hand some child's hand to pull
A steep hill
Huffing as she ascended
That day's entirety turned to sorrow

절망

북관(北關)에 계집은 튼튼하다
북관(北關)에 계집은 아름답다
아름답고 튼튼한 계집은 있어서
흰 저고리에 붉은 길동을 달어
검정치마에 받쳐입은 것은
나의 꼭 하나 즐거운 꿈이였드니
어늬 아침 계집은
머리에 무거운 동이를 이고
손에 어린것의 손을 끌고
가펴러운 언덕길을
숨이 차서 올라갔다
나는 한종일 서러웠다

The Things I Think

Outside in the season of a spring thaw in the pleasing warm night
The street may yet thrive, booming with people come out
Without knowing why, I wish to wander intimately about with such
people this night

However, upon this white mattress,[1] I look upon thin forearms
With bright blue veins, I ponder my having a poor father
That the maiden I'd longed for was wed
And the occasion of a close caring companion abandoning me

I ponder too, those people I know to be healthy in body and wealth
Coming and going to drink in happiness
My hand having not even one newly published book
And having no phonograph to hear even 'Aseora Saesangsa'[2]

And as I ponder, thoughts like these make hot the circles round my
eyes
And all around my heart.

1 A Korean-style mattress or 'yo' (요) is a thick cotton blanket/mat laid out on the floor
   like a futon with a lighter blanket on top for warmth.
2 Aseora Saesangsa (아서라 세상사(世上事)) is a reformed folk song meaning 'No World
   Affair' about a transient life, where life is like a daydream – so we should enjoy drinking.

내가 생각하는 것은

밖은 봄철날 따디기의 누굿하니 푹석한 밤이다
거리에는 사람두 많이 나서 흥성흥성 할 것이다
어쩐지 이 사람들과 친하니 쌔다니고 싶은 밤이다

그렇것만 나는 하이얀 자리 위에서 마른 팔뚝의
샛파란 핏대를 바라보며 나는 가난한 아버지를 가진것과
내가 오래 그려오든 처녀가 시집을 간 것과
그렇게도 살틀하든 동무가 나를 버린 일을 생각한다

또 내가 아는 그 몸이 성하고 돈도 있는 사람들이
즐거이 술을 먹으려 다닐것과
내 손에는 신간서(新刊書) 하나도 없는것과
그리고 그 '아서라 세상사(世上事)'라도 들을
유성기도 없는 것을 생각한다

그리고 이러한 생각이 내 눈가를 내 가슴가를
뜨겁게 하는 것도 생각한다

Looking Away Like This

Looking away like this, I walk the road, since the climate of a tranquil breeze is so sweet
   Since my poor companion has passed by in new shoes, since I forever wear the selfsame necktie and love one fair being

Looking away like this, I walk the road, also since I'm thankful for my meager salary
   Since at this early age, I attempt to grow a mustache and since the talk of delicious red gurnard[1] pan seared in strong soy sauce reaches some poor kitchen

1   The red gurnard (달재 생선) is a type of spiny bottom-dwelling redfish with a large head and eyes.

내가 이렇게 외면하고

　　내가 이렇게 외면하고 거리를 걸어가는 것은 잠풍 날씨가 너무나 좋은
탓이고
　　가난한 동무가 새 구두를 신고 지나간 탓이고 언제나 꼭 같은 넥타이를
매고 고운 사람을 사랑하는 탓이다

　　내가 이렇게 외면하고 거리를 걸어가는 것은 또 내 많지 못한 월급이
얼마나 고마운 탓이고
　　이렇게 젊은 나이로 코밑수염도 길러보는 탓이고 그리고 어느 가난한 집
부엌으로 달재 생선을 진장에 꼿꼿이 지진 것은 맛도 있다는 말이 자꾸 들려
오는 탓이다

The Joy of the Dark Round Shellfish

On the street of the dark round shellfish
I came to receive some rays of sun
With the sunshine not yet grown
The shellfish and I all are cold
Walking on the cold shaded side of this cold street
My heart is proud for that pleasure, proud
In some corner of this cold world
With one pure and poor friend
That I, like this passed down this cold street
How glad and clapping
Neatly lying with hand locked pillow
To curse louder and louder this lousy bastard's world

가무래기의 악(樂)

가무락조개 난 뒷간거리에
빛을 얻으려 나는 왔다
빛이 안 되어 가는 탓에
가무래기도 나도 모도 춥다
추운 거리의 그도 추운 능당 쪽을 걸어가며
내 마음은 웃즐댄다 그 무슨 기쁨에 웃즐댄다
이 추운 세상의 한 구석에
맑고 가난한 친구가 하나 있어서
내가 이렇게 추운 거리를 지나온 걸
얼마나 기뻐하며 낙단하고
그즈런히 손깍지베개하고 누어서
이 못된 놈의 세상을 크게 크게 욕할 것이다

Palwon[1]

On a frigid morning
The bus bound for Myohyang Mountain, hollow and vacant
A little lass ascends
Dressed in a jeogori,[2] as clean and green as that old expression
The back of her hands brittle and broken as a field's furrows
That little lass as she said making her way to Jaseong City
Jaseong that was 350-li from here and Myohyang Mountain 150-li
away[3]
Her cousin lives somewhere on Myohyang Mountain she said
Beyond the crystal white windows of the frozen bus
Giving an impression of a native territory commander,[4] an adult and
two youth await her
The arrival of that whimpering lass
In a corner of the hollow emptiness in that bus, some lone person
sheds a tear
That sad lass some several years at that native territory commander's
house
Cooking rice and washing rags and looking after those youngsters
Even on such a cold morning with hands frozen hard
Washing rags in icy water

---

1   Palwon (팔원(八院)) is a village in northern Korea.

2   Jeogori (저고리) is a half jacket of the traditional Korean hanbok dress.

3   350 li (리) is about 150 km or 115 miles. 150 li is about 70 km or 50 miles.

4   Native (내지인(內地人)) here refers to a Japanese person during the occupation.

팔원 (八院)

차디찬 아침인데
묘향산행(妙香山行) 승합자동차(乘合自動車)는 텅하니 비어서
나이 어린 계집아이 하나가 오른다
옛말속 가치 진진초록 새 저고리를 입고
손잔등이 밭고랑처럼 몹시도 터졌다
계집아이는 자성(慈城)으로 간다고 하는데
자성(慈城)은 예서 삼백오십리(三百五十里) 묘향산(妙香山) 백오십리(百五十里)
묘향산(妙香山) 어디메서 삼촌이 산다고 한다
새하야케 얼은 자동차(自動車) 유리창 밖에
내지인(內地人) 주재소장(駐在所長) 같은 어른과 어린아이 둘이 내임을 낸다
계집아이는 운다 느끼며 운다
텅 비인 차(車)안 한구석에서 어느 한 사람도 눈을 씻는다
계집아이는 몇 해고 내지인(內地人) 주재소장(駐在所長) 집에서
밥을 짓고 걸레를 치고 아이보개를 하면서
이러케 추운 아침에도 손이 꽁꽁 얼어서
찬물에 걸레를 첫슬 것이다

173

From the North

to Jung Hyun Woong

Long ago, I left
The northern realms of Buyeo, Suksin, Balhae, YeoJin, Yo, Geum
Heungan ridge, the mild slopes of Eum mountain, the Amureu
River banks, Sunggari stream
Abandoned the tiger, deer, raccoons
Broke faith with the flathead mullet, the catfish, and frogs, and I left

Looking back
I remember still the sorrowful birch and bowed coniferous cries
I've not forgotten the whispering of reed and wind to wait
When the Orochon sent me off with a farewell feast of wild boar[1]
And the Solon cried out along the road for ten li, I did not forget[2]

Looking back
No one could overcome such grief
Leaving lazily, I simply made my way
Soon thereafter, into the warm sunlight wearing white and eating
well-heaped rice
Sipping sweet spring water and dozing in daylight
Was startled by a distant dog's bark in the night
And bowed to every single passer by
Not even recognizing my remorse

In that time, headstones had cracked, many silver and gold treasures
been buried, and even crows had bred bloodlines

---

1   The Orochon (오로촌) were a nomadic tribe of Manchuria.
2   The Solon (쏠론) were a tribe of the Amureu River banks.

So when this new history had been built

Now driven by such overwhelming sorrow and grief

So even though I returned to my ancient sky, my age-old earth – my
placental place

The sun already old, the moon so pale, the wind unhinged, the
purple clouds floating aimless and alone

Ah, my ancestors, and siblings, and close kin, my neighbors

Those things I missed, that I loved, those things I looked up to, and
what I was proud of, my strength all waning

Like wind, water and time gone by

북방(北方)에서

정현웅(鄭玄雄)에게

아득한 옛날에 나는 떠났다

부여(扶餘)를 숙신(肅愼)을 발해(勃海)를 여진(女眞)을 요(遼)를 금(金)을

흥안령(興安嶺)을 음산(陰山)을 아무우르를 숭가리를

범과 사슴과 너구리를 배반하고

송어와 메기와 개구리를 속이고 나는 떠났다

나는 그때

자작나무와 이깔나무의 슬퍼하든 것을 기억한다

갈대와 장풍의 붙드든 말도 잊지 않었다

오로촌이 멧돌을 잡어 나를 잔치해 보내든 것도

쏠론이 십리길을 따러나와 울던 것도 잊지 않었다

나는 그때

아무 이기지 못할 슬픔도 시름도 없이

다만 게을리 먼 앞대로 떠나 나왔다

그리하야 따사한 햇귀에서 하이얀 옷을 입고 매끄러운 밥을

먹고 단샘을 마시고 낮잠을 잦다

밤에는 먼 개소리에 놀라나고

아침에는 지나가는 사람마다에게 절을 하면서도

나는 나의 부끄러움을 알지 못했다

그동안 돌비는 깨어지고 많은 은금보화는 땅에 묻히고 가마귀도 긴 족보를

이루었는데

이리하야 또 한 아득한 새 옛날이 비롯하는 때

이제는 참으로 이기지 못할 슬픔과 시름에 쫓겨

나는 나의 옛 하늘로 땅으로 - 나의 태반(胎盤)으로 돌아왔으나

이미 해는 늙고 달은 파리하고 바람은 미치고 보래구름
만 혼자 넋없이 떠도는데

아, 나의 조상은 형제는 일가친척은 정다운 이웃은
그리운 것은 사랑하는 것은 우러르는 것은 나의 자랑은 나의 힘은 없다
바람과 물과 세월과 같이 지나가고 없다

A Poem of Pumpkin Flower Lanterns

The heavens
Love chicks chirping near the reed fence.
Love crickets under the well stones.
And also
Love the poet who hee-haws like the donkey under the willow tree.

The heavens
Love mushrooms wearing conical hats and living in grass shadows.
Love shellfish living in the sand who lock their doors.
And also
Love the poet who lives lighting pumpkin flower lanterns under the
thick thatched roof.

The heavens
Love white clouds drifting in air.
Love streams flowing hidden through the valley.
And also
Love the poet who on the quiet, cozy countryside road only dreams
of gleaming sunshine.

The heavens
Have more love for the kind of poet who stays among us
Even though the whole world does not know this kind of poet, it is
all right
And still
Only calves and honey bees know the name of Kang So-cheon.[1]

---

1 Kang So-cheon (姜小泉) was well-known as a master of juvenile fiction in his time.

호박꽃 초롱 서시

한울은
울파주 가에 우는 병아리를 사랑한다.
우물돌 아래 우는 돌우래를 사랑한다.
그리고 또
버드나무 밑 당나귀 소리를 임내내는 시인을 사랑한다.

한울은
풀 그늘 밑에 삿갓 쓰고 사는 버섯을 사랑한다.
모래 속에 문 잠그고 사는 조개를 사랑한다.
그리고 또
두툼한 초가지붕 밑에 호박꽃 초롱 혀고 사는 시인을 사랑한다.

한울은
공중에 떠도는 흰 구름을 사랑한다.
골짜구니로 숨어 흐르는 개울물을 사랑한다.
그리고 또
아늑하고 고요한 시골 거리에서 쟁글쟁글 햇볕만 바래는 시인을 사랑한다.

한울은
이러한 시인이 우리들 속에 있는 것을 더욱 사랑하는데
이러한 시인이 누구인 것을 세상은 몰라도 좋으나
그러나
그 이름이 강소천인 것을 송아지와 꿀벌은 알 것이다.

A Return to the Farm

In the midst of Baekgudun field's melting snow, amid the thaw of its
earth-plowed field
  Standing with Master Rho, wealthy in land
  On the row's ridge where willows blossom
  Warm toasty rays, a calm quiet breeze
  I was entrusted with a rice paddy from landowner Master Rho   .

  Master Rho's horses, donkeys, ducks, and chickens swarm the house
  His storage room crammed, potatoes, beans and grains brimming
  Rather than struggle for the harvest Master Rho would listen to the
song of birds
  So he granted me a field today
  Now I grow sick of frivolous surveys and trivial records
  Would rather set aside my mind, dally and doze for a spell in the
daylight

  Such weather as I've never seen, clear and clean
  The clamor and thaw of melting snow, the ceaseless chatter of
budding willows
  At village edge horses, pigs, chickens, dogs and beasts whinny and
whine
  And the children and adults on the road and in the garden all abuzz
in the hubbub
  My heart infused with fervor, I delight in the stir and storm
  This spring I'll endeavor to sow and grow potato, corn, watermelon,
cucumber, peanuts, garlic, and green onions.
  When watermelons ripen, I will eat watermelon and sell them
  When the potatoes ripen, I will eat potatoes and sell them

If magpies, crows, moles or beetles come to eat them, leave them to eat

If thieves carry some off, let them carry it off

Ah Master Rho, this is the way I think

I look at Master Rho smiling as I speak.

Thus Master Rho feels free haven given the field

I, having gained the field, am at ease

Crunch-crunching through snow, plodding and placing soil

The sun's rays diamond bright tickling the nape of my neck

Master Rho folds his arms and strolls the field's ridge and furrow

I amble the furrows my hands clasped behind my back

Out of the field, around the outer rim, across the ditch, along the road

Pointing the way to a village of rooftops, of walled windbreaks and fences lit with beams of bright rays,

Master Rho on his donkey leads

And I follow on my mule

Along the road to the burial mounds of Chungwang at village end[1] to visit the spirit of Chungwang

And to find the tomb of Toshin to visit the spirit of Toshin[2]

---

1 Chungwang (충왕묘 (蟲王廟)) is a god that protects from harmful insects at harvest.

2 ToShin (토신묘 (土神廟)) is an Earth god responsible for fertile land.

귀농 (歸農)

백구둔(白狗屯)의 눈 녹이는 밭 가운데 땅 풀리는 밭 가운데
촌부자 노왕(老王)하고 같이 서서
밭두둑에 즘부러진 땅버들의 버들개지 피여나는 데서
볕은 장글장글 따사롭고 바람은 솔솔 보드라운데
나는 땅임자 노왕(老王)한테 석 상디기 밭을 얻는다

노왕은 집에 말과 나귀며 오리에 닭도 우울거리고
고방엔 그득히 감자에 콩 곡식도 들여 쌓이고
노왕은 채매도 힘이 들고 하루 종일 백령조(百鈴鳥) 소리나 들으려고
밭을 오늘 나한테 주는 것이고
나는 이제 귀치않은 측량(測量)도 문서(文書)도 싫증이 나고
낮에는 마음놓고 낮잠도 한잠 자고 싶어서
아전 노릇을 그만두고 밭을 노왕(老王)한테 얻는 것이다.

날은 챙챙 좋기도 좋은데
눈도 녹으며 술렁거리고 버들도 잎 트며 수선거리고
저 한쪽 마을에는 말 돼지에 닭 개 즘생도 들떠들고
또 아이 어른 행길에 뜨락에 사람도 웅성웅성 흥성거려
나는 가슴이 이 무슨 흥에 벅차오며
이 봄에는 이 밭에 감자 강냉이 수박에 오이며 당콩에 마눌과 파도
심그리라 생각한다.

수박이 열면 수박을 먹으며 팔며
감자가 앉으면 감자를 먹으며 팔며
까막까치나 두더쥐 돌벌기가 와서 먹으면 먹는 대로 두어두고
도적이 조금 걷어가도 걷어가는 대로 두어두고
아, 노왕(老王), 나는 이렇게 생각하노라
나는 노왕(老王)을 보고 웃어 말한다.

이리하여 노왕(老王)은 밭을 주어 마음이 한가하고
나는 밭을 얻어 마음이 편안하고
디퍽디퍽 눈을 밟으며 터벅터벅 흙도 덮으며
사물사물 햇볕은 목덜미에 간지로워서
노왕(老王)은 팔짱을 끼고 이랑을 걸어
나는 뒤짐을 지고 고랑을 걸어
밭을 나와 밭뚝을 돌아 도랑을 건너 행길을 돌아
지붕에 바람벽에 울타리에 볕살 쇠리쇠리한 마을을 가르치며
노왕(老王)은 나귀를 타고 앞에 가고
나는 노새를 타고 뒤에 따르고
마을 끝 충왕묘(蟲王廟)에 충왕(蟲王)을 찾어뵈려 가는 길이다
토신묘(土神廟)에 토신(土神)도 찾어뵈려 가는 길이다.

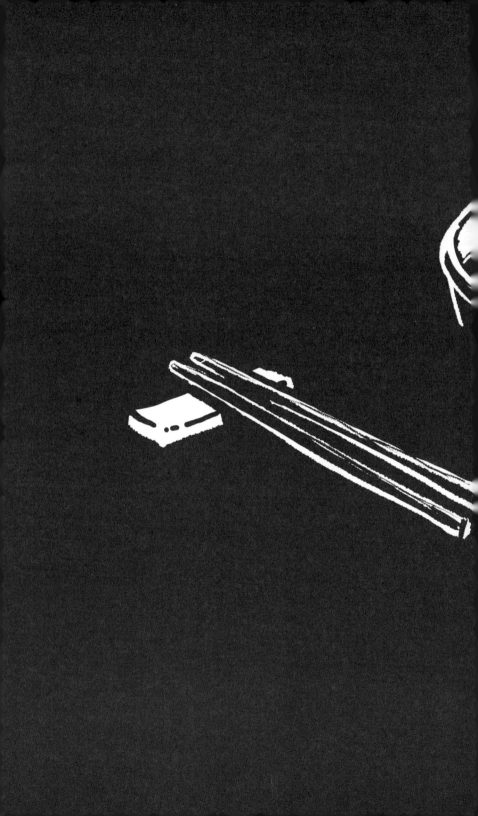

The Palatal & Pastoral
맛과 향과 전원시

Poems of Village, Community & Shaman Tradition
마을, 사회와 무속 문화

Herbal Medicine

Snow falls

In the earthen room over a ceramic heater in a shiny stone pot
medicine boils

Ginseng, sookbyun,[1] mokdan,[2] baekbokryung,[3] hemp root, and
taeksa root in a six flavor broth to build the body.

In the medicine pot as steam rises the slightly sweet fragrant smell
issues forth

Even the sound of boiling 'bbi-bbi' brings joy

And the remedy entirely infused is strained into a white drinking
bowl

As if ten thousand years of the past were infused in its distant
darkness

With two hands I calmly lift the medicine bowl and if I ponder the
people who conceived it

My heart becomes endlessly silent and clear

---

1 Sookbyun (숙변), or sookjihwang is herbal medicine that is steamed nine times and dried
   nine times.

2 Mokdan (목단), actually refers to the skin of the root of a mokdan plant.

3 Baekbokryung (백복령) is a mushroom-like, parasitic pine root used to control sweat
   and urine.

탕약 (湯藥)

눈이 오는데
토방에서는 질화로 위에 곱돌탕관에 약이 끓는다
삼에 숙변에 목단에 백복령에 산약에 택사의 몸을 보한다는
육미탕(六味湯)이다
약탕관에서는 김이 오르며 달큼한 구수한 향기로운 내음새가 나고
약이 끓는 소리는 삐삐 즐거웁기도 하다

그리고 다 달인 약을 하이얀 약사발에 밭어놓은 것은
아득하니 깜하야 만년(萬年) 옛적이 들은 듯한데
나는 두손으로 고이 약그릇을 들고 이 약을 내인 옛 사람들을 생각하노라면
내 마음은 끝없이 고요하고 또 맑어진다

Scene of an Autumn Night

The cock called twice and yet
The inner room the big room a lamp lit the long night dim and
silent
The people all awake and mixed in murmur
Chopping dried pumpkin and mixed kimchi
Then mincing dried ginger and onions and seaweed and garlic

Dried radish leaves boiling in the comfortably warm room
The air spiced all fresh and lively

From somewhere outside waterfowl cawing
In the earth-floored room fresh bean tofu quietly curdled

추야일경 (秋夜一景)

닭이 두 홰나 울었는데
안방 큰방은 홰즛하니 당등을 하고
인간들은 모두 웅성웅성 깨여 있어서들
도가리며 석박디를 썰고
생강에 파에 청각에 마눌을 다지고

시래기를 삶는 훈훈한 방안에는
양념 내음새가 싱싱도 하다

밖에는 어데서 물새가 우는데
토방에선 햇콩두부가 고요히 숨이 들어갔다

Sunset

On the street it's market day
On market street old men pass by
Those old men
Horse faced tiger faced weasel faced
Pug nosed saddle knob nosed jar nosed
Every nose wore folded reading glasses
Quartz framed reading glasses turtle-shell framed reading glasses
celluloid framed reading glasses[1]
The old men eyes glossed like windows
Raising a clamor of crude boorish Bukguan banter
Glaring bright in the setting sun
And like fierce beasts disappeared

1   The description uses Japanese pronunciation.

석양 (夕陽)

거리는 장날이다
장날 거리에 영감들이 지나간다
영감들은
말상을 하였다 범상을 하였다 쪽재비상을 하였다
개발코를 하였다 안장코를 하였다 질병코를 하였다
그 코에 모두 학실을 썼다
돌테 돋보기다 대모테 돋보기다 로이도 돋보기다
영감들은 유리창 같은 눈을 번득거리며
투박한 북관(北關) 말을 떠들어대며
쇠리쇠리한 저녁해 속에
사나운 즘생같이들 사러졌다

Hometown

As I lay alone afflicted in Bukgwan

One morning a doctor examined me

The doctor, his face like the generous Yeorae[1] and hanging with

Gwangong's beard[2]

From the remote past like a hermit of another land

His hand stretched out with the nail of his little finger outgrown

And in a length of stony silence took my pulse[3] of humors

Suddenly he asked of my hometown

It's called Pyungan-do Jungju

Then that's so-and-so's hometown

Then do you know so-and-so

The doctor drew a grin across his face

The best of friends, he said as he stroked his beard

I respect him as my father

The doctor smiled softly

Without a word he took my wrist and felt my pulse

The touch of his hand was warm and soft

My hometown and my father and my father's friend were all there

---

1 Yeorae (여래) is a kindhearted Buddhist god or possibly even Buddha himself.

2 Gwangong (관공), a mighty Chinese general of the "Record of the Three Kingdoms" who was well respected by Koreans.

3 Maeg (맥) or pulse of humors is a method of diagnosis in Chinese medicine

고향 (故鄕)

나는 북관(北關)에 혼자 앓아누워서
어느 아침 의원(醫員)을 뵈이었다.
의원은 여래(如來)같은 상을 하고 관공(關公)의 수염을 드리워서
먼 옛적 어느 나라 신선 같은데
새끼손톱 길게 돋은 손을 내어
묵묵하니 한참 맥을 짚더니
문득 물어 고향이 어데냐 한다
평안도 정주라는 곳이라 한즉
그러면 아무개 씨 고향이란다.
그러면 아무개 씨 아느냐 한즉
의원은 빙긋이 웃음을 띠고
막역지간이라며 수염을 쓴다.
나는 아버지로 섬기는 이라 한즉
의원은 또 다시 넌즈시 웃고
말없이 팔을 잡아 맥을 보는데
손길은 따스하고 부드러워
고향도 아버지도 아버지의 친구도 다 있었다.

Grandma's house

The house of my mounting fear

When at early evening filling the inner and outer courtyard flapping
and fluttering soft northern swallows beaked white with butterfly
beards gathering in constant coos jjang jjang jjang jjang came their
incessant metallic cries

Something in the night throwing small stones to the line of roof
between the tiles hanging bright a row of papered lamps from the pear
tree inside the back fence taking all the pots big and small from the
budumak[1] simply–simply pressing down upon the nape of someone's
neck ramming them down below the wooden slats

And at around dawn the storeroom shelf once piled neatly with
wooden bowls steamers and dippers are fallen strewn about the
earthen floor this house

---

1 A cooking fireplace, or budumak (부뚜막), is a traditional earthen platform in which an
iron pot for cooking rice is embedded and under which the fire is tended.

외갓집

내가 언제나 무서운 외갓집은

초저녁이면 안팎마당이 그득하니 하이얀 나비수염을 물은 보득지근한

복쪽재비들이 씨굴씨굴 모여서는 쨍쨍쨍쨍 쇳스럽게 울어대고

밤이면 무엇이 기와골에 무리돌을 던지고 뒤우란 배나무에 쩨듯하니

줄등을 헤여달고 부뚜막의 큰솥 적은솥을 모조리 뽑아놓고 재통에 간 사람의

목덜미를 그냥그냥 나려 눌러선 잿다리 아래로 처박고

그리고 새벽녘이면 고방 시렁에 채국채국 얹어둔 모랭이 목판 시루며

함지가 땅바닥에 넘너른히 널리는 집이다

Dogs

Lighting cow-fat on plate's rim, or caster oil in its bull-horn lamp, in the village on this winter's night, I welcome the sound of a dog's barking

On this fearful night as the town crier comes round the village, the dog barks

Somewhere at noontime, a pheasant or something caught, the man goes over the mountain to get noodles from the noodle factory, the dog barks

In this kimchi pot, dongchimi,[1] this notably delicious fermenting night.

Whenever daddy went to get noodles for a midnight meal, I sat wearing nana's spectacles and listened for the dog's barking.

1 Dongchimi (동치미) is radish kimchi in water served cold and refreshing.

개

접시 귀에 소기름이나 소뿔등잔에 아즈까리 기름을 켜는 마을에서는 겨울 밤 개 짖는 소리가 반가웁다

이 무서운 밤을 아래웃방성 마을 돌아 다니는 사람은 있어 개는 짖는다

낮배 어니메 치코에 꿩이라도 걸려서 산(山) 너머 국 수집에 국수를 받으러 가는 사람이 있어도 개는 짖는다

김치 가재미선 동치미가 유별히 맛나게 익는 밤

아배가 밤참 국수를 받으려 가면 나는 큰마니의 돋보 기를 쓰고 앉어 개 짖는 소리를 들은 것이다

The Tiger-like Great Aunt of the House Beyond the Hill

Above the yellow earth, on an elm tree mottled and colorful
rainbow-striped cloth in worn out scraps and hemp pieces hang,
attached with small straw bags and small straw bundles, and ripening
with loosely woven mourning sandal-like straw sandals,[1] going over
Kooksu shrine[2] pass how many times I spat sputtering,[3] in the valley a
house heavy with pillars and rafters ancient and old is embraced

In this house the white-haired dog-like geese always gaggling riotous
and unruly, horse-like dogs bark wildly and a male calf meanders amid
the savory-sweet smell of cow manure

In the house were dads and uncles, aunts and moms, with a suckling
babe laid in the shade of the village all day long, wearing a bamboo hat
went to weed the fields, as when the children got smallpox, chickenpox
and measles from what Jongaji[4] source unknown, on the passing road
the dead bodies of children rolled into pieces of straw mat, inside how
envious we were,[5] and at mealtime as many gourd dippers as children
lined the budumak[6] placed in an array with sticky-soft lumps of rice
in spoons to spoon and serve fed them, always talking of those things
again and again

---

1   The loosely woven straw sandals (엄신 같은 끈) are worn only for funerals.

2   Kooksu (국수) is a tutelary deity or guardian spirit.

3   One might spit (춤을 뱉고) in Korea likely for fear of ghosts.

4   Jongaji (종아지) is a ghost or diety that causes disease.

5   Envious (부러워) here, presumably because they were too poor to feed all their children.

6   A cooking fireplace or budumak (부뚜막) is a traditional earthen platform in which an
    iron pot for cooking rice is embedded and under which the fire is tended.

With the whole household fears the tiger-like great aunt, the children and grandchildren maggot-like squirming whipped with deulmae[7] tree switches bundled in the corners of the room and whipped with cow leather soles tied to bush clover whips

As I went on mom piggyback, like a wild horse bawling, pleading and pestering, in the height of blooming peony flower breaking off the lower stem, cutting a branch to give me with even an offering pear from its trunk and placing a prized goose egg in both hands

Because when my mother was carrying me, this great aunt one night dreamt of a colossal tiger coming to our ancestors' burial grounds, since my mom came from Seoul for marriage and moreover I was born as her nephew's first grandson, so she was pleased and proud of me

7   The deulmae tree (들매나무) is a manchurian ash.

넘언집 범 같은 노큰마니

황토 마루 수무나무에 얼럭궁 덜럭궁 색동헝겊 뜯개조박 뵈짜배기 걸리고
오쟁이 끼애리 달리고 소삼은 엄신같은 딥세기도 열린 국수당고개를 몇
번이고 튀튀 춤을 뱉고 넘어가면 골안에 아늑히 묵은 영동이 무겁기도 할
집이 한 채 안기었는데

집에는 언제나 셴개 같은 게사니가 벅작궁 고아내고 말 같은 개들이 떠들썩
짖어대고 그리고 소거름 내음새 구수한 속에 엇송아지 히물쩍 너들씨는데

집에는 아배에 삼춘에 오마니에 오마니가 있어서 젖먹이를 마을 청능
그늘 밑에 삿갓을 씌워 한종일내 뉘어두고 김을 매려 다녔고 아이들이 큰
마누래에 작은 마누래에 제구실을 할 때면 좋아지물본도 모르고 행길에 아이
송장이 거적뙈기에 말려나가면 속으로 얼마나 부러워하였고 그리고 깨때에는
부뚜막에 바가지를 아이덜 수대로 주룬히 늘어놓고 밥 한덩이 질게 한술
들여틀여서는 먹였다는 소리를 언제나 두고두고 하는데

일가들이 모두 범같이 무서워하는 이 노큰마니는 구덕살이같이
욱실욱실하는 손자 증손자를 방구석에 들매나무 회채리를 단으로 쩌다 두고
따리고 싸리갱이에 갓 신창을 매여놓고 따리는데

내가 엄매 등에 업혀가서 상사말같이 향약에 야기를 쓰면 한창 피는
함박꽃을 밑가지채 꺾어주고 종대에 달린 제물배도 가지채 쩌주고 그리고 그
애끼는 게사니알도 두 손에 쥐어주곤 하는데

우리 엄매가 나를 가지는 때 이 노큰마니는 어느 밤 크나큰 범이 한 마리
우리 선산으로 들어오는 꿈을 꾼 것을 우리 엄매가 서울서 시집을 온 것을
그리고 무엇보다도 내가 이 노큰마니의 당조카의 맏손자로 난 것을 대견하니
알뜰하니 기꺼이 여기는 것이었다

A Tale of Tinkling

On a long, lazy spring day, after playing with fire,[1] that night a story
of peeing, laying and peeing, flowing down the thigh, as a flavor of
warm and wet, to savor the wet and the warm

In first summer, after a hurried meal, when everyone comes out
front, peeing on clusters of cucumbers and soybeans, garden and street
permeating with pungent and smoky scents

On a long, lingering winter night, when all the people are asleep,
in the middle of the night I awake alone and pee endlessly into the
chamber pot at the head of the bed, tinkle and trickle, dribble and
drop

And according to mom, when I was still unaware of stale rice,[2] my
youngest aunt would wash her face with my pee,[3] the color vivid and
clear like dewdrops

---

1 Playing with fire (벌불 작난), in Korea, mothers would forbid their children to play with
the fire, telling them that playing with fire would cause them to wet their beds at night.

2 Still unaware of stale rice (아직 굳은 밥을 모르던) implies 'when I was still unable to
chew stale rice', when you feed a baby in Korea, you don't let it chew bread.

3 A baby's pee (오줌) was regarded as a health-giving drink in India and facial cleansing
lotion in Korea at the time.

동뇨부 (童尿賦)

봄철날 한종일내 노곤하니 벌불 작난을 한 날 밤이면 으례히 싸개동당을
지나는데 잘망하니 누어 싸는 오줌이 넙적다리를 흐르는 따끈따끈한 맛
자리에 평하니 괴이는 척척한 맛

첫 녀름 일은 저녁을 해치우고 인간들이 모두 터앞에 나와서 물외포기에
당콩 포기에 오줌을 주는 때 터 앞에 밭마당에 샛길에 떠도는오줌의 매캐한
재릿한 내음새

긴 긴 겨울밤 인간들이 모두 한잠이 들은 재밤중에 나 혼자 일어나서
머리맡 쥐밭 같은 새끼 오강에 한없이 누는 잘 매럽던 오줌의 사르릉 쪼로록
하는 소리

그리고 또 엄매의 말엔 내가 아직 굳은 밥을 모르던 때 살갗
퍼런망내고무가 잘도 받어 세수를 하였다는 내 오줌 빛은 이슬같이
샛맑앟기도 샛맑았다는 것이다.

Bukshin[1]

The smell of buckwheat in the street.

That smell of buckwheat, of an elder proper and pious to Buddha

On that street near the Hyangsan Buddha[2] of course the noodle
house hangs a sow like a shelf and the pork boasts hair like matting
needles for noodles

I gape at this unplucked pork

Watching people gulping slabs of unplucked meat, I sit and eat
black, buckwheat noodles

Suddenly, a warm feeling overcomes me

King Sosurim and King Gwangaeto come to mind

1 Bukshin (북신(北新)) is a small village in
   Pyunganbuk-do.

2 The Hyangsan Buddha (향산(香山)부처님)
   is located in Pohyonsa Temple in Hyangsan,
   North Pyongan, North Korea.

북신 (北新)

거리에서는 모밀내가 낫다
부처를 위하는 정갈한 노친네의 내음새 가튼 모밀내가 낫다

어쩐지 향산(香山)부처님이 가까웁다는 거린데 국수집에서는 농짝
가튼 도야지를 잡어걸고 국수에 치는 도야지고기는 돗바늘 가튼 털
이 드믄드믄 백엿다
나는 이 털도 안 뽑은 도야지 고기를 물구럼이 바라보며
또 털도 안 뽑는 고기를 시껌언 맨모밀국수에 언저서 한입에 꿀꺽
삼키는 사람들을 바라보며
나는 문득 가슴에 뜨끈한 것을 느끼며
소수림왕(小獸林王)을 생각한다 광개토대왕(廣開土大王)을 생각한다

Wooden Bowls[1]

In this huge house of five generations in the dim corner of the
dilapidated storage room
In close quarters with a rice pot, a trellis of wooden hooks, a sharp
wet stone, a stepping-stone for shoes, memories of old times, and
twelve guardian spirits

Several times a year at rites for distant ancestors, I come out from
the dim storage room and by the hand of the oldest Jegwan,[2] bald and
wearing a ceremonial horsehair hat, I symbolically cleanse my body.
And on the humble linden-tree table under the bright candles in front
of the memorial tablet on the long-legged chair I politely give some
soup with the wooden plate, Sikhye,[3] Sanjeok,[4] Namul,[5] fish and fruits,
and watch the bows and cup handling of the distant descendants, also
I love the mournful wails and written prayer, later I face the spirits
who've come to eat the food behind closing doors

The spirits, humans, souls, lives, something living, and something
dead, a handful of dirt, a handful of flesh, the sacred, dim sorrow of
the distant ancestors and descendants are frozen in time

---

1 Moggu (목구(木具)) is a set of wooden bowls used exclusively for ancestor worship
   rituals.
2 Jegwan (제관) is a person charged with officiating the ritual process for ancestor worship
   ceremonies.
3 Sikhye (식혜) is a cold, sweet traditional desert drink made with barley malt powder and
   rice.
4 Sanjeok (산적) is a pan-fried skewer of seasoned slices of beef with vegetables.
5 Namul (나물) refers to a variety of edible grass or leaves or seasoned herbal dishes made
   of them.

With my grandson's grandson and my grandson, with my grandfather, my grandfather's grandfather, and my grandfather's grandfather.... And the sorrow like the moon like a night like a rain like an ox's blood like a bear like a tiger, who is strong and sturdy but wise and friendly, of the Baek Family of Suwon and the Baek village of Jungju are frozen in time

목구 (木具)

오대(五代)나 내린다는 크나큰 집 다 찌그러진 들지고방 어득시근한
구석에서 쌀독과 말쿠지와 숫돌과 신뚝과 그리고 옛적과 또 열두 데석님과
친하게 살으면서

한 해에 몇 번 매연지난 먼 조상들의 최방등 제사에는 컴컴한 고방 구석을
나와서 대멀머리에 외얏맹건을 지르터 맨 늙은 제관의 손에 정갈히 몸을 씻고
교의 우에 모신 신주 앞에 환한 촛불 밑에 피나무 소담한 제상 위에 떡 보탕
식혜 산적 나물 지짐 반봉 과일들을 공손하니 받들고 먼 후손들의 공경스러운
절과 잔을 굽어보고 또 애끊는 통곡과 축을 귀애 하고 그리고 합문 뒤에는
흠향 오는 구신들과 호호히 접하는 것

구신과 사람과 넋과 목숨과 있는 것과 없는 것과 한줌 흙과 한 점 살과 먼
옛 조상과 먼 훗 자손의 거룩한 아득한 슬픔을 담는 것

내 손자의 손자와 손자와 나와 할아버지와 할아버지의 할아버지와
할아버지의 할아버지의 할아버지와…… 수원 백씨(水原白氏) 정주
백촌(定州白村)의 힘세고 꿋꿋하나 어질고 정 많은 호랑이 같은 곰 같은 소
같은 피의 비 같은 밤 같은 달 같은 슬픔을 담는 것 아 슬픔을 담는 것

Watermelon Seed, Pumpkin Seed

Coming to a country where the virtuous are many
Learning the heart and handiwork of those benevolent souls
Sorting watermelon seeds, pumpkin seeds with my front teeth

Putting watermelon seeds, pumpkin seeds in my mouth, the idea
In fact foolish, juvenile and lazy
Yet indeed bright, intense, deep and heavy
With a full heart, full of times gone by, full of ancient wisdom
And full of the long absence of humanity's nest
Smeared across the clouds of Mount Taishan[1] and the water of the
Yellow River, the virtue of the earth and trees of old kings, can be
seen in this full heart

These little, light, longish white and black seeds
Muted and mature, up and down from hand to mouth, mouth to
hand
Hoping to hear birds singing afield and taking a geomungo[2] to play
a tune,
Leaving five thousand seeds behind, hoping to cross Hangu pass[3]
As my heart fills with happiness shelling white and black seeds with
my front teeth, I become a monkey
As sadness sinks in holding white and dark seeds between teeth at
tongue's end, I become a magpie

---

1 Mount Taishan (태산(泰山)) is an historically and culturally significant sacred mountain
located North of the city of Tai'an, in Shandong province, China.

2 A geomungo (거문고) is a six stringed Korean zither.

3 Hangu Pass or Hanguguan (함곡관(函谷關)), literally 'enveloped valley,' the pass
separates the upper Yellow River and Wei valleys.

In a country brimming with benevolent minds

To the person tossing aside a small bag of rice[4] and coming below

the willow tree

In his pocket, there must be something sorting watermelon seeds,

sorting pumpkin seeds

To the person eating edible greens and drinking water, hands behind

his head laying back

At the top of this head, there must be a thing sorting watermelon

seeds, sorting pumpkin seeds

4　Odumi (오두미(五斗米)) is a small bag of rice that represents a small salary of
government official.

수박씨, 호박씨

어진 사람이 많은 나라에 와서
어진 사람의 짓을 어진 사람의 마음을 배워서
수박씨 닦은 것을 호박씨 닦은 것을 입으로 앞니빨로 밝는다

수박씨 호박씨 입에 넣는 마음은
참으로 철없고 어리석고 게으른 마음이나
이것은 또 참으로 밝고 그윽하고 깊고 무거운 마음이라
이 마음 안에 아득하니, 오랜 세월이 아득하니, 오랜 지혜가
또 아득하니 오랜 인정(人精)이 깃들인 것이다
태산(泰山)의 구름도 황하(黃河)의 물도 옛임금의 땅과 나무
의 덕도 이 마음 안에 아득하니 뵈이는 것이다

이 작고 가벼웁고 갤족한 희고 까만 씨가
조용하니 또 도고하니 손에서 입으로 입에서 손으로 오르나리는 때
벌에 우는 새소리도 듣고 싶고, 거문고도 한 곡조 뜯고 싶고,
한 오천(五千)말 남기고 함곡관(函谷關)도 넘어가고 싶고
기쁨이 마음에 뜨는 때는 희고 까만 씨를 앞니로 까서 잔나비가 되고
근심이 마음에 앉는 때는 희고 까만 씨를 혀끝에 물어 까막까치가 되고

어진 사람이 많은 나라에서는
오두미(五斗米)를 버리고 버드나무 아래로 돌아온 사람도
그 넓차개에 수박씨 닦은 것은 호박씨 닦은 것은 있었을 것이다
나물 먹고 물 마시고 팔베개하고 누었던 사람도
그 머리맡에 수박씨 닦은 것은 호박씨 닦은 것은 있었을 것이다

Heo Jun[1]

From the country of the clear and sacred tears, he comes
From the country of warm, bright sunlight, he comes

You who come from the land of tears and sunshine
Come for an outing in this world
Come for some solitary excursion

A man from the land of tears and sunshine
You with that long bent waist, hands clasped behind your back,
weary legs
When you cross the crowded street, chock-full of bellicose
bargaining booming loud
One wintry night, sitting by the head of a poor friend who lay sick
I suppose as you sit silent, petting a kitten on your knee
In your peaceful heart and on the edge of your eye
As the clear sky arises in your country
On your azure forehead, your crooked shoulders
The brush of the nap of your nation's warm breeze as you pass
As if on a towering summit of a high mountain
If not, deep, the water deep, your nation's land lies low
How clear and high the sky
How warm and fragrant the breeze
And under this sky, unfurled through the feel of the breeze
How fine and fair those customs, compassion and language

But one long-necked poet knows

---

1 Heo Jun (허준 (許俊)) was a contemporary of Baek Seok, a short story writer and
intimate friend.

Even when Dostoyevsky and Joyce wrote such familiar, notable
novels
Behaving as if knowing nothing of it, enjoying the dark of lazing in
the room

To the beloved child begrudging a single piece of taffy and in
devotion to your wife dressing her in threadbare clothes
To poor-hearted unfamiliar folk handing out hundreds of yang^2 in
change so warmhearted and such words
That people will lose everything and gain a soul, such a grave saying

That distant land of tears and sunshine
This person who came for an outing in this world
This long-necked poet again with the clamor of a chatty goose
You who smile sadly as you pull out a paduk board

2 The yang (양 (兩)) was the currency of Korea between 1892 and 1902.

215

허준 (許俊)

그 맑고 거룩한 눈물의 나라에서 온 사람이여
그 따사하고 살틀한 볕살의 나라에서 온 사람이여

눈물의 또 볕살의 나라에서 당신은
이 세상에 나들이를 온 것이다
쓸쓸한 나들이를 단기려 온 것이다

눈물의 또 볕살의 나라 사람이여
당신이 그 긴 허리를 굽히고 뒤짐을 지고 지치운 다리로
싸움과 흥정으로 와자지껄하는 거리를 지날 때든가
추운 겨울밤 병들어 누운 가난한 동무의 머리맡에 앉어
말없이 무릎 우 어린 고양이의 등만 쓰다듬는 때든가
당신의 그 고요한 가슴 안에 온순한 눈가에
당신네 나라의 맑은 한울이 떠오를 것이고
당신의 그 푸른 이마에 삐어진 어깻죽지에
당신네 나라의 따사한 바람결이 스치고 갈 것이다
높은 산도 높은 꼭대기에 있는 듯한
아니면 깊은 물도 깊은 밑바닥에 있는 듯한 당신네 나라의
하늘은 얼마나 맑고 높을 것인가
바람은 얼마나 따사하고 향기로울 것인가
그리고 이 하늘 아래 바람결 속에 퍼진
그 풍속은 인정은 그리고 그 말은 얼마나 좋고 아름다울 것인가

다만 한 목이 긴 詩人은 안다
'도스토엡흐스키'며 '죠이스'며 누구보다도 잘 알고 일등가는 소설도 쓰지만
아무것도 모르는 듯이 어드근한 방안에 굴어 게으르는 것을 좋아하는 그
풍속을
사랑하는 어린것에게 엿 한 가락을 아끼고 위하는 안해에겐 해진 옷을

216

입히면서도

　마음이 가난한 낯설은 사람에게 수백냥 돈을 거져 주는 그 인정을 그리고
또 그 말을

　사람은 모든 것을 다 잃어버리고 넋 하나를 얻는다는 크나큰 그 말을

　그 멀은 눈물의 또 볕살의 나라에서

　이 세상에 나들이를 온 사람이여

　이 목이 긴 詩人이 또 게사니처럼 떠곤다고

　당신은 쓸쓸히 웃으며 바둑판을 당기는구려

217

Noodle Soup

As snow fell fast

The mountain bird flutters downward to the grassy meadow

As the hare plunges into hidden snow hollows

In the village, what a welcome thing awaits.[1]

The children unfettered, hunt pheasants in the coming darkness.

The poor mother heads for the kimchi hut in the mid of night

The village, seeming savory, brimming with pleasure and excitement, all aflutter, quiet in the growing din, heady and high, it is coming.

This thing, from the edge of some sunny or some shady place, some isolated mountain slope

All night milk-white steam placed on plate's edge mingles with beef tallow burning in the kitchen haze

Like some dragon[2] riding the noodle maker, it comes.

This thing from the distant past, a standard of unhurried and happy times gone by

Like a thread through a spring rain, through the burning hot summer, through a sweet gust of autumn,

Through generation after generation, through birth and death and death and birth, through the growing hearts of the people of this village, through their blurred dreams,

On the roof, in the yard, on the skirt of the well, fat flakes of snow amass, such a night,

In front of father, in front of the young son, in front of father a big bowl, in front of the son a small bowl, a full spool is coming.

---

1   In this case, the 'welcome thing' (반가운 것이) alludes to a pleasant smell, ostensibly of the noodle soup.

2   Traditional Korean Dragons (산멍에) were thought to look like snakes.

This thing, as if that great grandma who rode the bear's back, the bear who had raised her,

As if she that stood and sneezed on that straw mat when he heard from that village over the mountain, from that distant time as if that great grandpa that raced to her side,[3] it comes.

This pale, soft, plain, subtle thing, what is it?

On this winter night, with impeccably ripened radish-water kimchi, with that beautifully biting red-pepper powder, with that flavorful fresh pheasant

And that smell of smoke, that smell of vinegar, and that smell of boiled beef boiled in beef broth, the smell that fills the reed-matted room with the spit and seethe of boiling, that warm welcoming spot near the fired floor, what is that?

This tranquil village, this village of well-mannered inhabitants, this close-knit place, what is it?

This unquestionably classy but simple thing, what is this?

3 This story of the great grandpa (먼 옛적 큰아버지) comes from an old Korean fable.

국수

눈이 많이 와서
산엣새가 벌로 나려 멕이고
눈구덩이에 토끼가 더러 빠지기도 하면
마을에는 그 무슨 반가운 것이 오는가 보다
한가한 애동들은 어둡도록 꿩사냥을 하고
가난한 엄매는 밤중에 김치가재미로 가고
마을을 구수한 즐거움에 사서 은근하니 흥성흥성 들뜨게 하며 이것은 오는
것이다.
이것은 어늬 양지귀 혹은 능달쪽 외따른 산 옆 은댕이 예데가리 밭에서
하룻밤 뽀오얀 흰 김 속에 접시귀 소기름불이 뿌우연 부엌에
산멍에 같은 분틀을 타고 오는 것이다.
이것은 아득한 옛날 한가하고 즐겁던 세월로부터
실 같은 봄비 속을 타는 듯한 여름 속을 지나서 들쿠레한 구시월 갈바람
속을 지나서
대대로 나며 죽으며 죽으며 나며 하는 이 마을 사람들의 의젓한 마음을
지나서 텁텁한 꿈을 지나서
지붕에 마당에 우물 둔덕에 함박눈이 푹푹 쌓이는 여느 하룻밤
아배 앞에 그 어린 아들 앞에 아배 앞에는 왕사발에 아들 앞에는
새끼사발에 그득히 사리워오는 것이다.
이것은 그 곰의 잔등에 업혀서 길러났다는 먼 옛적 큰 마니가
또 그 집등색이에 서서 자채기를 하면 산 넘엣 마을까지 들렸다는 먼 옛적
큰아버지가 오는 것같이 오는 것이다.
아, 이 반가운 것은 무엇인가.
이 히수무레하고 부드럽고 수수하고 슴슴한 것은 무엇인가.
겨울밤 쩡하니 닉은 동치미국을 좋아하고 얼얼한 댕추가루를 좋아하고
싱싱한 산꿩의 고기를 좋아하고

그리고 담배 내음새 탄수 내음새 또 수육을 삶는 육수국 내음새 자욱한

220

더북한 삿방 쩔쩔 끓는 아르굴을 좋아하는 이것은 무엇인가.

이 조용한 마을과 이 마을의 의젓한 사람들과 살뜰하니 친한 것은 친한
것은 무엇인가.

이 그지없이 고담(枯淡)하고 소박(素朴)한 것은 무엇인가.

Fauna & Flora
동식물상

Poems of the Natural World & the Passage of Time
자연계와 시간의 흐림

Ducks

Duck on a night near the ChungMyung[1] you're fond of
Even if someone slaps your cheek it's too dark to see it coming
Duck the time of Spring thaw by evening's end is dark

Even though you ducks enjoy the night so much, how boisterous
you wander about in the fields by the sea
Having visited that land by the sea grandma said in complaint
That the ducklings as if on a market day rush were clamorous and
noisy

Even so duck going on the silent road at night
Near rice paddy plots from whence
When 'gga-al gga-al' your sounds of gaiety spring
I am joyed as if hearing 'jiggol jiggol' the gabbling of friends from
my village
Duck even I want to join your round of talking
To brighten the night together

Duck I like you I like you so
Beside the rice paddy I lay out the unripe rice still hanging from
withered stalks
And bury the straw rope to a chicken feathered snare
And hide beyond the embankment
To spend the day in waiting for you

---

1 ChungMyung (청명 (清明)) is one of twenty-four traditional Korean days that mark the
seasons that signifies the warming of Spring—in March or April.

Duck fair duck keep calm in my arms
That old man sells you and drinks in the liquor market
That widower cow acupuncturist old man
I buy you for a white nickel

Thinking of me the Mudang's daughter gave my young sister
You pair of ducks
My young sister gone that daughter alas married off
Ducks you pair are flying away

오리

오리야 네가 좋은 청명(淸明) 밑께 밤은
옆에서 누가 뺨을 쳐도 모르게 어둡다누나
오리야 이때는 따디기가 되여 어둡단다

아무리 밤이 좋은들 오리야해변벐에선 얼마나 너이들이 욱자지껄하며
벡이기에
  해변땅에 나들이 갔던 할머니는
  오리새끼들은 장꽁이나 하듯이 떠들썩하니 시끄럽기도 하드란 숭인가

그래도 오리야 호젓한 밤길을 가다
가까운 논배미들에서
까알까알 하는 너이들의 즐거운 말소리가 나면
나는 내 마을 그 아는 사람들의 지껄지껄하는 말소리같이 반가웁고나
오리야 너이들의 이야기판에 나도 들어
밤을 같이 밝히고 싶고나

오리야 나는 네가 좋구나 네가 좋아서
벌논의 옆에 쭈구렁 벼알 달린 짚검불을 널어놓고
닭이 올코에 새끼달은치를 묻어놓고
동둑넘에 숨어서
하로진일 너를 기다린다

오리야 고은 오리야 가만히 안겼거라
너를 팔어 술을 먹는 노(盧)장에 영감은
홀아비 소의연 침을 놓는 영감인데
나는 너를 백동전 하나 주고 사오누나

나를 생각하던 그 무당의 딸은 내 어린 누이에게
오리야 너를 한쌍 주드니
어린 누이는 없고 저는 시집을 갔다건만
오리야 너는 한쌍이 날어가누나

The Mill

Even the moonbeams, even the beggar, even the stray dog are
pleased all
Even the winnower, even the dairy cow, even the rake of light, all
cheerful

The thieving cat's claws extend and
The fattened weasel sprouts to stretch long

The hen in the roost lays an egg and cries
The puppy eats chaff and pees

The dogs gather to play-fight
Let loose the piglet caught and carried in a water jug embrace

A calf plays properly and
The magpie incessantly barks

The wedding procession horse nays as he goes
The market donkey too calls as he goes

As above the rafters, even a loom, even a window shade, even a
cotton gin[1], all cozy
As from corner to corner, even a plow, even a plowshare, even the
raking light all cozy

---

1   A torigae (토리개) is a tool used to remove the seeds from cotton plants, similar to the
    cotton gin.

연자간

달빛도 거지도 도적개도 모다 즐겁다
풍구재도 얼럭소도 쇠드랑볕도 모다 즐겁다

도적괭이 새끼락이 나고
살진 쪽제비 트는 기지개 길고

홰냥닭은 알을 낳고 소리 치고
강아지는 겨를 먹고 오줌 싸고

개들은 게모이고 쌈지거리하고
놓여난 도야지 동구재벼 오고

송아지 잘도 놀고
까치 보해 짖고

신영길 말이 울고 가고
장돌림 당나귀도 울고 가고

대들보 위에 베틀도 채일도 토리개도 모도들 편안하니
구석구석 후치도 보십도 소시랑도 모도들 편안하니

Yellow Day

If you walk about ten li more, they say there's a village with a temple. The rays of slanted daylight have the warmth of a satiny sheen. The earth heaped-high like a breast full of flesh, it must be unbearable so deep in the haze. Inside the back fence, the house with the peach blossoms blooming must be empty. That empty house with pheasants flying to and fro. A flock of thrushes perch atop an old ash outside of fence. Chasing white clouds and hunting beetles, maybe because of their love for verdant leaves brought them to rest there. Even on the edge of the field peach blossoms blossom. Even a new bride blossoms. A new bride peach blossom. A peach blossom bride. Somewhere mae— a calf cries. In a vegetable garden on the ridge between rice paddies stepping on water celery,[1] I stand crying. Just go under the peach tree and play in the dirt why cry. On an embankment at the end of the field not going anywhere your mama lays there. Scared by the sound of a horse whinny from the lower village, rather a foal would fear your sound in the lower village. To take a cat nap and then to wash its face. On the path as the white clouds cross the facing mountain standing and gazing at peach blossoms. A squirrel peering at the facing mountain grumbling, so titillating.

Over there shadows upon shadows, over here sun-sunshiny—
Over there shadows upon shadows, over here sun-sunshiny—

---

1 Oenanthe javanica (미나리) is commonly called Chinese celery, water celery or water dropwort.

230

황일 (黃日)

한 십리(十里) 더 가면 절간이 있을 듯한 마을이다. 낮 기울은 볕이
장글장글하니 따사하다. 흙은 젖이 커서 살같이 깨서 이지랑이 낀 속이
안타까운가 보다. 뒤울 안에 복사꽃 핀 집엔 아무도 없나 보다. 뷔인 집에
꿩이 날어와 다니나 보다. 울밖 늙은 들매남에 튀튀새 한불 앉었다. 흰구름
따러가며 딱장벌레 잡다가 연두빛 닢새가 좋아 올라왔나 보다. 밭머리에도
복사꽃 피었다. 새악시도 피었다. 새악시 복사꽃이다. 복사꽃 새악시다. 어데서
송아지 매─하고 운다. 골갯논드렁에서 미나리 밟고 서서운다. 복사나무
아래 가 흙장난하며 놀지 왜 우노. 자개밭둑에 엄지 어데 안 가고 누었다.
아릇동리선가 말 웃는 소리 무서운가, 아릇동리 망아지 네 소리 무서울라.
담모도리 바윗잔등에 다람쥐 해바라기하다 조은다. 토끼잠 한잠 자고 나서
세수한다. 흰구름 건넌산으로 가는 길에 복사꽃 바라노라 섰다. 다람쥐 건넌산
보고 부르는 푸념이 간지럽다.

저기는 그늘 그늘 여기는 챙챙─
저기는 그늘 그늘 여기는 챙챙─

231

A Bunting's Call[1]

Pollacks dry at eave's edge

The pollack frozen in stiff semblance

The pollack lean and longish

At tail's end longish icicles hung

As the sun grows dark and the day goes by, the somber rays become cold

I too am a lean and longish pollack

Frozen in stiff semblance at door's edge

From my heart longish icicles hung

1 A small seed-eating songbird related to the finch, with a
short stout bill and usually brown or gray feathers.
Family: Emberizidae

멧새소리

처마끝에 명태를 말린다
명태는 꽁꽁 얼었다
명태는 길다랗고 파리한 물고긴데
꼬리에 길다란 고드름이 달렸다
해는 저물고 날은 다 가고 볕은 서러웁게 차갑다
나도 길다랗고 파리한 명태다
문턱에 꽁꽁 얼어서
가슴에 길다란 고드름이 달렸다

The Evening of Bakkaksi's Coming[1]

After an evening meal of rice cooked with beans, eggplant and cold
soup
As the bakkaksi and juraksi[2] fly up all aflutter to the roof white with
gourd blossoms
All the house doors opened up and empty
The humans ascend the back hill[3] and spread a straw mat to feel the
breeze
In the grass field, a load of white laundry is hung unnoticed
The crickets and grasshoppers shake the mountainside chirping
shrill and sharp
Thereupon the stars in the sky were like beans in the yard and
As if from a night of rain the kidney bean field filled with dew

1   A bakkaksi (박각시) or brown convolvulus hawk-moth, is literally translated as a gourd's
    bride implying the moth that pollinates a gourd's flower.
2   A juraksi (주락시) is a type of striped julgaksi moth.
3   Koreans believe a house should have a river to its southern front and a mountain (뒷등성)
    to its northern back.

박각시 오는 저녁

당콩밥에 가지 냉국의 저녁을 먹고 나서
바가지꽃 하이얀 지붕에 박각시 주락시 붕붕 날아오면
집은 안팎 문을 횅 하니 열젖기고
인간들은 모두 뒷등성으로 올라 멍석자리를 하고 바람을 쐬이는데
풀밭에는 어느새 하이얀 다림질감들이 한불 널리고
돌우래며 팟중이 산옆이 들썩하니 울어댄다
이리하여 한울에 별이 잔콩 마당 같고
강낭밭에 이슬이 비 오듯 하는 밤이 된다

Andong

On this foreign thoroughfare
Fog falls like rain
The falling rain falls like fog

On this foreign thoroughfare
The scent of soybean oil brewing
The smell of boiling bondi[1]

On this foreign thoroughfare
The keen cut of axe to grinding wheel in your sound
The music of a Chinese clown playing Yanggeum[2]

I fancied cultivating long, confident nails and donning a long trailing
Chinese jacket
I fancied wearing a conical hat and chewing a pipe
If conceivable, I would chomp and chew on fragrant pear and ride a
two-horse carriage with a lady with long hanging hair

---

1   Bondi (번디) is dialect for beondegi (번데기) is a popular Korean street food of steemed
    silkworm pupae.

2   A yanggeum (되앙금) is a traditional Korean string instrument like a hammered
    dulcimer.

안동 (安東)

이방(異邦) 거리는
비 오듯 안개가 나리는 속에
안개 가튼 비가 나리는 속에

이방(異邦) 거리는
콩기름 쪼리는 내음새 속에
섭누에 번디 삶는 내음새 속에

이방(異邦)거리는
독기날 별으는 돌물네 소리 속에
되광대 켜는 되앙금 소리 속에

손톱을 시펄하니 길우고 기나긴 창꽈쯔를 즐즐 끌고 시펏다
만두(饅頭) 꼭깔을 눌러쓰고 곰방대를 물고 가고 시펏다
이왕이면 향(香)내 노픈 취향리(梨) 돌배 움퍽움퍽 씹으며 머리채
츠렁츠렁 발굽을 차는 꾸냥과 가즈런히 쌍마차(雙馬車) 몰아가고 시
펏다.

237

DoAn at HamNam[1]

At this small depot, Gowonseon line's last station,
The clang-clang streetcar blustering boastfully as it hurtles forward
Stands solitary, vacant and plaintive
The sunlight like a hanging lantern twinkles bright

On the clean, sandy platform
Everyone, sip and slurp, drinks nutty boiled oat straw tea
Where the spirited splash and spray of arctic lamprey resound

To reach that lake

I must cross the limitless field with its bunches of bog bilberries

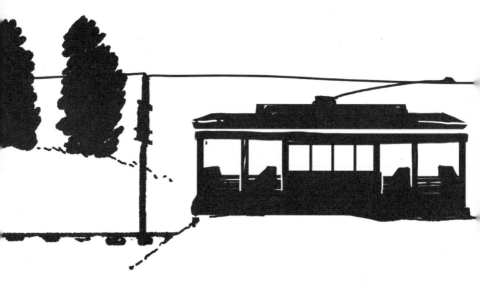

1   DoAn (도안) is a small town in Hamgyeong Namdo (함남) South Hamgyong Province,
    North Korea, where the terminal station of the Highland Line.

함남도안 (咸南道安)

고원선(高原線) 종점인 이 작은 정차장엔
그렇게도 우쭐대며 달가불시며 뛰어오던 뽕뽕차가
가이없이 쓸쓸하니도 우두머니 서 있다
해빛이 초롱불같이 히맑은데

해정한 모래부리 플랱폼에선
모두들 절절 끓는 구수한 귀이리차(茶)를 마신다
칠성(七星)고기라는 고기의 쩜벙쩜벙 뛰노는 소리가

쨋쨋하니 들려오는 호수까지는

들쭉이 한불 새까마니 익어가는 망연한 벌판을 지나가야 한다

Gujang Road
Poem of a trip to the West 1

3-li[1] distant on those riverside rocks

My rain-drenched clothes now nearly downy and dry on the road,
returning

Yet around another mountain bend, my clothes drenched again

I've heard that I can get to the road by walking 20-li

Yet even after a great distance, still out of sight

I ponder of a beautiful maid I had met on some hidden mountain
trail

As I recall that massive one-ja[2] mandarin fish I spotted in a random
stretch of river

Through mountain rain, my clothes wet and dry, I return

Now growling hungry

So when I arrive at the road where the a clay vessel peddler stops by,

If nothing else, let's go to that place with the 'spirits shop' sign
posted

That cozy heated stone floor

And that siraegi[3] soup with ox's blood added, boiled with tofu, that
warm slow savory hangover soup

A few bowls, a few grand bowls and a few more, let's eat

1 3 li (리) would be about 1.5km or one mile.

2 One ja (자) equals 30cm (11.8 inches).

3 Siraegi (시래기) soup is made with dried radish leaves and stems.

구장로 (球場路)
서행시초 (西行詩抄) 1

삼리(三里) 밖 강(江)쟁변엔 자갯돌에서
비멀이한 옷을 부숭부숭 말려입고 오는 길인데
산(山)모롱고지 하나 도는 동안에 옷은 또 함북 젖었다

한 이십리(二十里) 가면 거리라든데
한것 남아 걸어도 거리는 뵈이지 않는다
나는 어니 외진 산길에서 만난 새악시가 곱기도 하던것과
어니메 강물 속에 들여다 뵈이든 쏘가리가 한자나 되게 크던 것을 생각하며
산(山)비에 젖었다는 말렀다 하며 오는 길이다

이젠 배도 출출히 고팠는데
어서 그 옹기장사가 온다는 거리로 들어가면
무엇보다도 몬저 '주류판매업(酒類販賣業)'이라고 써붙인 집으로 들어가자

그 뜨수한 구들에서
따끈한 삼십오도(三十吾度) 소주(燒酒)나 한잔 마시고
그리고 그 시래기국에 소피를 넣고 두부를 두고 끓인 구수한 술국을
뜨근히
몇 사발이고 왕사발로 몇 사발이나 먹자

Manchu Poems 만주시

A White Wind Wall

On this narrow stretch of partitioned wall papered white[1]
Only lonely things come and go somehow tonight

On this white wind wall
As the faint flickering fifteen-watt bulb throwing its weary light
across its barren face
Casting a dim shadow of a worn and tattered cotton shirt
And again I desire a draught of a sweet warm rice drink
With the wanderings of my lonesome thoughts
But then what is this business

On this white wind wall
Is my poor old mother
My poor old mother
On such a frozen day, her hands plunge, washing cabbage, in the
frigid water
Then again my love,
The adorable woman of my heart
In a far southern district, a hushed low-ceilinged house at estuary's
edge
She sits opposite her husband over a dinner of fish soup
But now a youngster too, appears in the fold
And again, in the deep of night, something separates

On this white wind wall
I stare at my lonely face

1 A 'white wind wall' (흰 바람벽) refers to a white wallpaper covering and the shadows
   passing by a visualization of the thoughts passing throught the mind of the poet.

244

And thus the words go by

— I, in this world of want and lonesome poverty, of supreme sorrow, was born to keep living

And this world continues on even though

My heart is filled with too much heat of desolation and love and sadness

As if this is the time I would be consoled and as if this is the time someone would join me

With quivering eyes and shaking fist as these words flicker by

— As heaven creates, He the most precious and rare things, makes all

Poor and alone and lofty and desolate and always overflowing with love and filled with inner sadness

Appearing in the likes of a crescent moon, a gourd flower, a mateless bluetit, a donkey

And also as if Francis Jammes, and Doe Youn Myung and Rainer Maria Rilke

흰 바람벽이 있어

오늘 저녁 이 좁다란 방의 흰 바람벽에
어쩐지 쓸쓸한 것만이 오고간다

이 흰 바람벽에
희미한 십오촉(十五燭) 전등이 지치운 불빛을 내어 던지고
때글은 낡은 무명 샷쯔가 어두운 그림자를 쉬이고
그리고 또 달디단 따끈한 감주나 한잔 먹고 싶다고 생각하는 내 가지가지
외로운 생각이 헤매인다
그런데 이것은 또 어인일인가

이 흰 바람벽에
내 가난한 늙은 어머니가 있다
내 가난한 늙은 어머니가
이렇게 시퍼러둥둥하니 추운 날인데 차디찬 물에 손은 담그고 무이며
배추를 씻고 있다
또 내 사랑하는 사람이 있다
내 사랑하는 어여쁜 사람이
어느 먼 앞대 조용한 개포가의 나즈막한 집에서
그의 지아비와 마주앉어 대구국을 끓여 놓고 저녁을 먹는다
벌써 어린것도 생겨서 옆에 끼고 저녁을 먹는다
그런데 또 이즈막하야 어느사이엔가

이 흰 바람벽엔
내 쓸쓸한 얼굴을 쳐다보며
이러한 글자들이 지나간다
— 나는 이 세상에서 가난하고 외롭고 높고 쓸쓸하니 살어가도록
태어났다
그리고 이 세상을 살어가는데

내 가슴은 너무도 많이 뜨거운 것으로 호젓한 것으로 사랑으로 슬픔으로
가득찬다
그리고 이번에는 나를 위로 하는 듯이 나를 울력 하는 듯이
눈질을 하며 주먹질을 하며 이런 글자들이 지나간다
— 하늘이 이 세상을 내일적에 그가 가장 귀해하고 사랑하는 것들은 모두
가난하고 외롭고 높고 쓸쓸하니 그리고 언제나 넘치는 사랑과 슬픔 속에
살도록 만드신 것이다
초생달과 바구지 꽃과 짝새와 당나귀가 그러하듯이
그리고 또 '프랑시스 쨈'과 '도연명'과 '라이넬 마리아 릴케'가 그러 하듯이

Child from the Countryside

Oh child from the countryside

Oh child who came from the countryside in that late-night
passenger car

Even in this cold, topped with some dried meadow foxtail jacket,
and nothing underneath, nearly naked

Oh child, something black on your cheek, crude and coarse, your
hair caked yellow

Oh child with your two plump and pillowy legs already putting on
power

This morning, what was it that startled you to make you sob so

Clearly, stunned by some false and futile thing

Such is the bitter sob of a pure and trusting heart

This house filled with so many others

All fierce with greed and violence, headstrong and deliberately
deafening

For such young souls, their cry is far too loud with inflated fear

Only, you sob soft instinctively stifling shrieks, restraining yourself

Your voice a bit hoarse and husky

Your voice makes my heart grow bright, burning hot and becoming
sunny

I want to hoist you up, stroke your hair, grasp your little hand and
shake it

The sound of your voice as evening meal is being made in a country
farmhouse

Sitting alone in a room full of sunshine

And thinking of a child grabbing some string and traditional socks
to play secretly

On a midsummer day, as every adult sets off for the fields, in the utterly empty earthen room

Bothered by a baby dog wagging, picking and eating chicken poop, thinking of such a child

Oh child from the countryside, this morning you sobbed bitterly for some reason

You will undoubtedly be a blessed poet or farmer

촌에서 온 아이

촌에서 온 아이여
촌에서 어제밤에 승합자동차(乘合自動車)를 타고 온 아이여
이렇게 추운데 웃동에 무슨 두룽이 같은 것을 하나 걸치고 아랫두리는 쪽
발가벗은 아이여
뽈다구에는 징기징기 앙광이를 그리고 머리칼이 놀한 아이여
힘을 쓸랴고 벌써부터 두 다리가 푸둥푸둥하니 살이 찐 아이여
너는 오늘 아츰 무엇에 놀라서 우는구나
분명코 무슨 거즛되고 쓸데없는 것에 놀라서
그것이 네 맑고 참된 마음에 분해서 우는구나
이 집에 있는 다른 많은 아이들이
모도들 욕심 사납게 지게굳게 일부러 청을 돋혀서
어린아이들 치고는 너무나 큰소리로 너무나 뤼겁많은 소리로 울어대는데
너만은 타고난 그 외마디소리로 스스로웁게 삼가면서 우는구나
네 소리는 조금 썩심하니 쉬인 듯도 하다
네 소리에 내 마음은 반끗히 밝어오고 또 호끈히 더워오고 그리고
즐거워온다
나는 너를 껴안어 올려서 네 머리를 쓰다듬고 힘껏 네 적은 손을 쥐고
흔들고 싶다
네 소리에 나는 촌 농사집의 저녁을 짓는 때
나주볕이 가득 드리운 밝은 방안에 혼자 앉어서
실감기며 버선짝을 가지고 쓰렁쓰렁 노는 아이를 생각한다
또 녀름날 낮 기운 때 어른들이 모두 벌에 나가고 텅 뷔인 집 토방에서
햇강아지의 쌀랑대는 성화를 받어가며 닭의똥을 주어먹는 아이를
생각한다
촌에서 와서 오늘 아츰 무엇이 분해서 우는 아이여
너는 분명히 하눌이 사랑하는 시인(詩人)이나 농사꾼이 될 것이로다

At the Bathhouse

I bathe like the people of China
As the descendants of Yin, Shang, or Yue[1]
Entering the same tub to soak
Each country with distinct individuals
Everyone utterly undressed, body by body melting together
Generation by generation of forebears unaware of each other,
discrete in language, the way of dressing and eating, all different
Thus, all together stripped bare, body by body bathing
If I think about it, seems isolating
All these people of differing nations all with smooth wide brows,
dark cloudy eyes and long legs all bare and hairless
Why should I be so often sad for it
But that person who left, halfway lying on the wood-board bench
Staring endlessly at southern sunbeams, seeming to delight in the
day by himself this long-necked man
Tao Yuanming would have been such a man[2]
And here sprinting to plunge into the hot water
As if some water bird with a caw-caw squawk, this wan gaunt man
The man called YangJa would have been such a man[3]
I now came to the ancient country of Qin or Wei
It seems I meet only people I like
In this way, somehow my heart suddenly feels welcome
Though I am growing somewhat scared and lonesome

---

1 Yin, Shang, or Yue (은(殷)이며 상(商)이며 월(越)이며) are names for different periods
and places in Chinese history: the Yin or Shang Dynasty, the State of Yu, etc.

2 Tao Yuanming (도연명(陶淵明)), 365-427 AD also known as Tao Qian or T'ao
Ch'ien, a Chinese poet considered to be one of the greatest poets of the Six dynasties
period.

3 Yangja (양자 (陽子) 440–360 BC) was a Chinese thinker and hedonist.

Nevertheless, in truth whether Yin, Shang, Yue,

Wei, or Qin, the people of such countries their descendants

How their hearts are idle and free

Forgetting to steep myself in hot water or scrub the dirt and dead skin

I merely peer at my navel or stare into the faces of others

Meanwhile I taste some 'Dance of the Swallow' swallow's nest soup

And some new bride somewhere so pure and pretty in my mind such a thing as I think

For me, such free idle minds that yet know how to love their way of living and spending life

Those profound and constant hearts are truly worthy of affection and admiration

Though the people, each of different countries

Well not even youngsters being utterly undressed

Seems somewhat silly

조당(澡塘)에서

나는 지나(支那)나라 사람들과 같이 목욕을 한다
무슨 은(殷)이며 상(商)이며 월(越)이며 하는 나라 사람들의 후손들과 같이
한 물통 안에 들어 목욕을 한다
서로 나라가 다른 사람인데
다들 쭉 발가벗고 같이 몸에 몸을 녹이고 있는 것은
대대로 조상도 서로 모르고 말도 제각금 틀리고 먹고 입는 것도 모두
다른데
이렇게 발가들 벗고 한 물에 몸을 씻는 것은
생각하면 쓸쓸한 일이다
이 딴 나라 사람들이 모두 이마들이 번번하니 넓고 눈은 컴컴하니 흐리고
그리고 길죽한 다리에 모두 민숭민숭하니 다리털이 없는 것이
이것이 나는 왜 자꾸 슬퍼지는 것일까
그런데 저기 나무판장에 반쯤 나가 누어서
나주볕을 한없이 바라보며 혼자 무엇을 즐기는 듯한 목이 긴 사람은
도연명(陶淵明)은 저러한 사람이었을 것이고
또 여기 더운 물에 뛰어들며
무슨 물새처럼 악악 소리를 지르는 삐삐 파리한 사람은
양자(陽子)라는 사람은 아모래도 이와 같었을 것만 같다
나는 시방 옛날 진(晉)이라는 나라나 위(衛)라는 나라에 와서
내가 좋아하는 사람들을 만나는 것만 같다
이리하야 어쩐지 내 마음은 갑자기 반가워지나
그러나 나는 조금 무서웁고 외로워진다
그런데 참으로 그 은(殷)이며 상(商)이며 월(越)이며
위(衛)며 진(晉)이며 하는 나라 사람들의 이 후손들은
얼마나 마음이 한가하고 게으른가
더운 물에 몸을 불키거나 때를 밀거나 하는 것도 잊어 버리고
제 배꼽을 들여다보거나 남의 낯을 쳐다보거나 하는 것인데
이러면서 그 무슨 제비의 춤이라는 연소탕(燕巢湯)이 맛도 있는 것과

또 어늬 바루 새악시가 곱기도 한 것 같은 것을 생각하는 것일 것인데
나는 이렇게 한가하고 게으르고 그러면서 목숨이라든가 인생이라든가 하는
것을 정말 사랑할 줄 아는
그 오래고 깊은 마음들이 참으로 좋고 우러러진다
그러나 나라가 서로 다른 사람들이
글쎄 어린아이들도 아닌데 쪽 발가벗고 있는 것은
어쩐지 조금 우스웁기도 하다

Together with Du Fu or Li Bai[1]

Today, on the first full moon of the new year

The year's lunar lantern festival

So far away from my hometown, in such a lonely place

Like those long-ago poets of this land, Du Fu or Li Bai

Being so far away, would have endured such a day

If I were at home today,

I would wear new clothes, new shoes, eat copious rice cakes and a feast of meat,

Family and relatives would gather to spend a day full of joy, sharing smiles,

But today, with long-worn, unclean clothes, a hunk of dried fish in hand

I sit alone amid muddled lonesome thoughts

Old poets of this realm, like Du Fu or Li Bai,

On such a day, with a hunk of dried fish, must have sat amid their muddled lonesome thoughts

Now a little place on an isolated street comes to mind, someone from my hometown

I guess I should stop by and buy a bowl of that place's delicious rice-cake soup to eat

As our ancestors have always done, generation after generation since the long-forgotten past

So too, poets like Du Fu or Li Bai as they stayed in foreign lands,

On such a day would seek out a tavern, an inn, of a person from same province,

---

1 Du Fu (두보(杜甫)), 712-770AD, a prominent Chinese poet of the Tang dynasty. Along with Li Bai (이백(李白)), 701-762 AD, they are frequently called the greatest of the Chinese poets, taking traditional poetic forms to new heights.

And as their ancestors had always done, as they would raise Lunar
rice cakes to lips,
Wouldn't their hearts find comfort, find rest in that
In doing so, these old poets of clear mind
In the distant future, their someday descendants
As part of their essence, on this day they would eat Lunar rice cakes
As they grew mournful,
I too would set my rice cake soup aside and brim with sorrow
Ah, this first full moon of the new year, it's lantern festival
On the street, fireworks blazing, burst and pop, the sound of
Chinese fiddle flowing,
In my lonely heart, the poets of this place, their past,
I often ponder their heavy hearts
Perhaps my lonesome heart is not dissimilar to the sentiments
people like Du Fu or Li Bai,
Still, such is the loneliness of the distant past

두보(杜甫)나 이백(李白)같이

오늘은 정월(正月) 보름이다
대보름 명절인데
나는 멀리 고향을 나서 남의 나라 쓸쓸한 객고에 있는 신세로다
옛날 두보나 이백 같은 이 나라의 시인도
먼 타관에 나서 이 날을 맞은 일도 있었을 것이다
오늘 고향의 내집에 있는다면
새 옷을 입고 새 신도 신고 떡과 고기도 억병 먹고
일가친척들과 서로 모여 즐거이 웃음으로 지날 것이런만
나는 오늘 때문은 입든 옷에 마른 물고기 한 토막으로
혼자 외로이 앉아 이것저것 쓸쓸한 생각을 하는 것이다
옛날 그 두보나 이백 같은 이 나라의 시인도
이날 이렇게 마른 물고기 한 토막으로 외로이 쓸쓸한 생각을 한 적도
있었을 것이다
나는 이제 어느 먼 외진 거리에 한고향 사람의 조그마한 가업집이 있는
것을 생각하고
이 집에 가서 그 맛스러운 떡국이라도 한 그릇 사먹으리라 한다
우리네 조상들이 먼먼 옛날로부터 대대로 이 날엔 으레히 그러하며 오듯이
먼 타관에 난 그 두보나 이백 같은 이 나라의 시인도
이 날은 그 어느 한고향 사람의 주막이나 반관(飯館)을 찾어가서
그 조상들이 대대로 하든 본대로 원소(元宵)라는 떡을 입에 대며
스스로 마음을 느꾸어 위안하지 않았을 것인가
그러면서 이 마음이 맑은 옛 시인들은
먼 훗날 그들의 먼 훗자손들도
그들의 본을 따서 이날에는 원소를 먹을 것을
외로이 타관에 나서도 이 원소를 먹을 것을 생각하며
그들이 아득하니 슬펐을 듯이
나도 떡국을 놓고 아득하니 슬플 것이로다
아, 이 정월(正月) 대보름 명절인데

거리에는 오독독이 탕탕 터지고 호궁(胡弓) 소리 삘삘 높아서
내 쓸쓸한 마음엔 작꼬 이 나라의 옛 시인(詩人)들이 그들의
쓸쓸한 마음들이 생각난다
내 쓸쓸한 마음은 아마 두보(杜甫)나 이백(李白) 같은 사람들의 마음인지도
모를 것이다
아무려나 이것은 옛투의 쓸쓸한 마음이다

Mountain

It is said it did not like it's hair combed
The lice rise up
To pull a hand of hair
Such a mountain

Crossing the mountain they say
Would-be commanders sprouting wings
Lived as braided bachelors
Shouldered young maidens well

If standing on the mountain top
In the distance always and forever flickering-flickering
On the shadow drawn mountain
A thunderbolt struck a large wildcat
To become a boulder
With stretched out whiskers looking across this thing looked fearful

But seeing past the flowered rock of sorrel[1] and azaleas blooming
red
The mountain side a site for gajichui[2] bbogugchoi[3] gaerugi[4]
fernbrake and other edible greens
The mountain strongly scented with wild edible greens
I bound after a northern roe

---

1   Rumex Acetosa (쉬영꽃), a perennial herb called spinach dock or narrow-leaved dock.

2   Aster scaber, or gajichui (가지취), is a perennial herb found in wild mountain regions of
    Korea, Russia, China and Japan, often used in herbal side dishes called namul (나물).

3   Rhaponticum uniflorum, or bbogugchoi (뻐국채), is a maral root of the thistle tribe
    within the sunflower family.

4   Platycodon, or gaerugi (계루기), balloon bellflower or Chinese bellflower.

산 (山)

머리 빗기가 싫다면
이가 들구 나서
머리채를 끄을구 오른다는
산(山)이 있었다

산(山) 너머는
겨드랑이에 깃이 돋아서 장수가 된다는
더꺼머리 총각들이 살아서
색씨 처녀들을 잘도 업어간다고 했다

산(山)마루에 서면
멀리 언제나 늘 그물그물
그늘만 친 건넌산(山)에서
벼락을 맞아 바윗돌이 되었다는
큰 땅꽹이 한 마리
수염을 뻗치고 건너다보는 것이 무서웠다

그래도 그 쉬영꽃 진달래 빨가니 핀 꽃바위 너머
산(山) 잔등에는 가지취 뻐국채 게루기 고사리 산나물판
산(山)나물 냄새 물씬물씬 나는데
나는 복장노루를 따라 뛰었다

Solitary Nature

In the cucumber field the time of withering cabbage
If you come to the mountain, the sound of the mountain
If you come to the plain, the sound of the plain

If you come to the mountain
In a wide pine grove, the cuckoo's call
In a modest pine grove, the ring-necked pheasant's call

If you come to the plain
On the rice paddy ridge, a sheldrake's call
In the reeds, the reed warbler's call

If you come to the mountain, the din of the mountain, in the
mountain I am alone
If you come to the plain, the spirited sound of the plain, I am alone

Jungju Tongrim about ninety ri[1] along the long, long day's road
If you come to the mountain, the sounds of the mountain if you
come to the plain, the sounds of the plain
I must be in solitary nature

1   One ri (리(里)) equals 393m so 90 ri is about 35,000m or 12 miles.

적막강산

오이 밭에 벌배채 통이 지는 때는
산에 오면 산 소리
벌로 오면 벌 소리

산에 오면
큰솔밭에 뻐꾸기 소리
잔솔밭에 덜거기 소리

벌로 오면
논두렁에 물닭의 소리
갈밭에 갈새 소리

산으로 오면 산이 들썩 산 소리 속에 나 홀로
벌로 오면 벌이 들썩 벌 소리 속에 나 홀로

정주(定州) 동림(東林) 구십(九十)여 리(里) 긴긴 하로 길에
산에 오면 산 소리 벌에 오면 벌 소리
적막강산에 나는 있노라

A Village of Apparitions

'Tis my lot to be born in such a village
A village of unnerving apparitions high and low
My ever-present fear stifles my five power practice[1]
In my room, the spirit of the house
If I withdraw to the dirt-floor for fear of that house spirit, the earth
spirit is there
For fear I advance to the kitchen, an ancestral ghost awaits

I escape to the storeroom to hide myself, again a shelf holds a
guardian spirit
This time to the corner ondol stack[2] I ran, there a giant ashen
apparition
In a frenzied fog of fatigue, I break for the back fence, there inside
the god of the jujube tree
With no alternative, I open the gate to go
There at the gate, the powerful guardian totems stand

I narrowly break free through the gate and bolt
Passing the millstone in the corner of the garden, here too a
millstone specter
In such a shutter, I set out on a wide well-trodden trail
Feeling free of worries, I amble on with an easy gait unguarded
Ah no, beyond belief at every turn an egg-shaped apparition hounds
my heels
An entire village teeming with ghosts, now I have nowhere to go

---

1 The Five Buddhist powers (오 력) - 1. Trust or Confidence 2. Chi (Energy)
   3. Mindfulness 4. Concentration (Mind for Enlightenment) 5. Wisdom

2 Ondol (온돌) is an infloor heating system common to Korea, indicated by goltong (굴통).

마을은 맨천 구신이 돼서

나는 이 마을에 태어나기가 잘못이다
마을은 맨천 구신이 돼서
나는 무서워 오력을 펼 수 없다
자 방안에는 성주님
나는 성주님이 무서워 토방으로 나오면 토방에는 다운구신
나는 무서워 부엌으로 들어가면 부엌에는 부뜨막에 조앙님

나는 뛰쳐나와 얼른 고방으로 숨어 버리면 고방에는 또 시렁에 데석님
나는 이번에는 굴통 모롱이로 달아가는데 굴통에는 굴대장군
얼혼이 나서 뒤울 안으로 가면 뒤울 안에는 곱새녕 아래 털능구신
나는 이제는 할 수 없이 대문을 열고 나가려는데
대문간에는 근력 세인 수문장

나는 겨우 대문을 삐쳐나 바깥으로 나와서
밭 마당귀 연자간 앞을 지나가는데 연자간에는 또 연자당구신
나는 고만 디겁을 하여 큰 행길로 나서서
마음 놓고 화리서리 걸어가다 보니
아아 말 마라 내 발뒤축에는 오나가나 묻어 다니는 달걀구신
마을은 온데간데 구신이 돼서 나는 아무데도 갈 수 없다

265

All Souls Day[1]

In the village, everyone to the field three times to weed and seed
After boiling and eating dog-stew three or four times
A fine day, this Festival of Souls comes quietly

On the day of the Festival of Souls, the new brides
Dress up in linen skirts, hemp skirts from Tianjin, skirts fluttering
above the knees,
Jeoksam jackets[2] from Suzhou, linen Jeoksam, Jeoksam with longish
purple breast-bows,
Thoroughly dressed in all the fine clothes one has for the outing

Three or four layers of traditional Korean wigs to adorn their heads
Pinning pigtails with long, narrow, red ribbons aslant
Barefoot in beautiful woven straw sandals
Crossing many passes to a mineral spring

In this hot, humid sear of summer, along the mud path
A soft swaying breeze comes cool
Carrying coin purse waist pockets finally filled with funds after so
long
Emerging from a bundle cloth, a silver knife, a needle kit, wooden
mandarin ducks, a 'go' stone

---

1 BaekJung (칠월백중) a Buddhist festival celebrated on the 15th of July by the lunar
calendar, called "All Souls Day" or the "Festival of Souls," in Korea it is more of an
agricultural holiday of supplication to the agricultural deities to ensure a bounteous
harvest in the coming autumn.

2 Jeoksam (적삼) is an unlined summer jacket or sleeved vest made of a single layer of
linen or hemp for traditional Korean hanbok.

Dazzling ornate tassels sounding swish-swish[3]
Crossing many passes to arrive at a mineral spring
At the spring, many crowd around wearing white

From our friend's place come folks we're glad to greet
Offering up powdered sesame gruel, Korean pancakes, the pine
powder rice cakes I bought to offer up and eating in front of our
breast-bows
Then caught in an All Souls Day shower, we raced away wet

This time, I'll not forget the trip to my friend's place even in my
dreams
Even on my way to my friend's place from close of July to early
Autumn
Considering an unhurried life at the house and
Reflecting on my cherished clothes even when wet, the rain only
seems refreshing

3 Seurerok-seurerok (스르럭스르럭) the sounds of flap and flutter or swish swish.

칠월백중

마을에서는 세불 김을 다 매고 들에서
개장취념을 서너 번 하고 나면
백중 좋은 날이 슬그머니 오는데
백중날에는 새악시들이
생모시치마 천진퉤치마의 물팩치기 껑추렁한 치마에
쇠주퉤적삼 항라적삼의 자지고름이 기드렁한 적삼에
한끝나게 상나들이옷을 있는 대로 다 내입고
머리는 다리를 서너 켜레씩 들어서
시뻘건 꼬둘채댕기를 삐뚜룩하니 해꽂고
네날백이 따배기신을 맨발에 바꿔 신고
고개를 몇이라도 넘어서 약물터로 가는데
무썩무썩 더운 날에도 벌 길에는
건들건들 씨언한 바람이 불어오고
허리에 찬 남갑사 주머니에는 오랜만에 돈푼이 들어 즈벅이고
광지보에서 나온 은장두에 바늘집에 원앙에 바둑에
번들번들하는 노리개는 스르럭스르럭 소리가 나고
고개를 몇이라도 넘어서 약물터로 오면
약물터엔 사람들이 백재일치듯 하였는데
붕가집에서 온 사람들도 만나 반가워하고
깨죽이며 문주며 섶자락 앞에 송구떡을 사서 권하거니 먹거니 하고
그러다는 백중 물을 내는 소내기를 함뿍 맞고
호주를하니 젖어서 달아나는데
이번에는 꿈에도 못 잊는 붕가집에 가는 것이다
붕가집을 가면서도 칠월 그믐 초가을을 할 때까지
평안하니 집살이를 할 것을 생각하고
애끼는 옷을 다 적시어도 비는 씨원만 하다고 생각한다

Park Si-bong's Place
(in Yudong, South Shinuiju)

With time's passage, I realize I lack a wife and also,
Lost is the house of our mutual habitation,
And my devoted parents and also my siblings fell to far off,
To the end of this some strong winded lonely road, I wander'd about.
Duly the day grows dark,
The wind blows still more strongly, a chill gradually gathers force,
In some carpenter's house, I lay out an old straw mat,
Entering one room of my host's lodging.
In this way, I in this damp smelling, cold moist room,
By day or night, thinking I, even alone am too much,
If a straw fire is piled in the pottery brazier,
As I hug it taking warmth to my hands, as I write meaningless words
in the ash
As well, I do not venture out and lie in my place,
A pillow of intertwined hands beneath my head and behaving this
way,
I chew my saddness, my foolishness, repeatedly as a cow ruminating.

When my heart chokes fast,
When a turn of searing tears gather in my eyes,
Again when thinking of my past disgrace, my face flushing shame
red,
There was a feeling I could not but die, pressed down in my saddness
and my foolishness.
But then in a moment I lifted my head,
When looking at the white window or again, opening my eyes to
stare at the high ceiling

At this time with my will, moreover my strength, I deem guiding myself to be arduous in industry and,

I think but because, more than these, there is a bigger, higher thing, rolling me on as it pleases,

As many days pass thus,

In my dizzy mind the sadness, the lamentation, the things that will settle to sediment gradually sink and

About when I have only lonely thoughts,

From time to time, toward evening pat-pat the pellet snow pelts the window,

On such an evening, I wrap myself tight around the stove and endeavor to bend my knees,

On the back slope of some distant mountain, standing lonely away from the boulders,

As darkness comes with the white snow showering, those drying leaves,

With a pat-pat the snow pelting,

That purportedly rare, firm and pure tree called Dahurian,buckthorn, of that tree I was pondering.

남신의주 유동 박시봉방
(南新義州柳洞朴時逢方)

어느 사이에 나는 아내도 없고, 또,
아내와 같이 살던 집도 없어지고,
그리고 살뜰한 부모며 동생들과도 멀리 떨어져서,
그 어느 바람 세인 쓸쓸한 거리 끝에 헤매이었다.
바로 날도 저물어서
바람은 더욱 세게 불고, 추위는 점점 더해 오는데,
나는 어느 목수네 집 헌 삿을 깐,
한 방에 들어서 쥔을 붙이었다.
이리하여 나는 이 습내 나는 춥고, 누긋한 방에서,
낮이나 밤이나 나는 나 혼자도 너무 많은 것 같이 생각하며,
딜옹배기에 북덕불이라도 담겨 오면
이것을 안고 손을 쬐며 재 위에 뜻없이 글자를 쓰기도 하며,
또 문밖에 나가지도 않고 자리에 누워서,
머리에 손깍지베개를 하고 구르기도 하면서,
나는 내 슬픔이며 어리석음이며를 소처럼 연하여 쌔김질하는 것이었다.

내 가슴이 꽉 메어 올 적이며,
내 눈에 뜨거운 것이 핑 괴일 적이며,
또 내 스스로 화끈 낯이 붉도록 부끄러울 적이며,
나는 내 슬픔과 어리석음에 눌리어 죽을 수밖에 없는 것을 느끼는
것이었다.
그러나 잠시 뒤에 나는 고개를 들어,
허연 문창을 바라보든가 또 눈을 떠서 높은 천장을 쳐다보는 것인데,

이때 나는 내 뜻이며 힘으로, 나를 이끌어가는 것이 힘든 일인 것을
생각하고,
이것들보다 더 크고, 높은 것이 있어서, 나를 마음대로 굴려가는 것을
생각하는 것인데,

이렇게 하여 여러 날이 지나는 동안에,

내 어지러운 마음에는 슬픔이며, 한탄이며, 가라앉을 것은 차츰 앙금이 되어 가라앉고

외로운 생각만이 드는 때쯤 해서는,

더러 나줏손에 쌀랑쌀랑 싸락눈이 와서 문창을 치기도 하는 때도 있는데,

나는 이런 저녁에는 화로를 더욱 다가 끼며, 무릎을 끓어 보며,

어느 먼 산 뒷옆에 바우섶에 따로 외로이 서서,

어두워 오는데 아이야니 눈을 맞을, 그 마른 잎새에는,

쌀랑쌀랑 소리도 나며 눈을 맞을,

그 드물다는 굳고 정한 갈매나무라는 나무를 생각하는 것이었다.

The Earthworm and I

Grew to serpent's size

For a thousand years, nightly adding water to clay, that clay a worm
created

Amid the monsoons from the sky, together with the rain they fall

To become bait for Prussian carp and river bass

In my science book, babies emerged from the confluence of a male
and a female

I wish to see the worm's eyes

I look on the worm's food and home with envious eyes

나와 지렁이

내 지렁이는
커서 구렁이가 되었읍니다.
천년 동안만 밤마다 흙에 물을 주면 그 흙이 지렁이가 되었읍니다.
장마지면 비와 같이 하늘에서 내려왔읍니다.
뒤에 붕어와 농다리의 미끼가 되었읍니다.
내 이과책에서는 암컷과 수컷이 있어서 새끼를 낳았읍니다.
지렁이의 눈이 보고 싶습니다.
지렁이의 밥과 집이 부럽습니다.

'I'm Drunk'

To Noritakae Gaseuo

I am drunk

I am drunk on old scotch

I am drunk on sadness

I am drunk on pondering the turn of happiness and on that ever
budding sadness

I am intoxicated with this night's still existence

'나 취했노라'
- 노리다께 가스오(則武三雄)에게 –

나 취했노라

나 오래된 스코틀랜드의 술에 취했노라

나 슬픔에 취했노라

나 행복해진다는 생각에 또한 불행해진다는 생각에 취했노라

나 이 밤의 허무한 인생에 취했노라

<原文>

われ 醉へり

われ 古き蘇格蘭土の酒に醉へり

われ 悲みに醉へり

われ 幸福なることまた不幸なることの思ひに醉へり

われ この夜空しく虚なる人生に醉へりス

277

Pomegranate

At the grassless southern edge of that sunny place, my hometown
Embracing the last rays of evening, sustained by sunset

Born long ago
Yet dreaming of becoming a virtuous person
On the old mountain glade, digging yams and returning

The moonlight, an unfamiliar place
The snow fall, a fight among spirits

석류

남방토 풀 안 돋은 양지귀가 본이다
햇비 멎은 저녁의 노을 먹고 산다

태고에 나서
선인도가 꿈이다
고산 정토에 산약 캐다 오다

달빛은 이향
눈은 정기 속에 어우러진 싸움

Loneliness

I walk with loneliness side-by-side
Whistling ho-ee-ho-ee[1]
Kicking dewdrops down the grassy trail on the outskirts of town

Suddenly, the past comes to mind — as I had grown fond of that
time
Among the pines at the back of the mountain one old tomb
Every night it welcomes us, so what of it!

At that time, not even once had we
Felt the least bit curious about what was buried inside that tomb
Even with the owl's hoots through the oak forest, we'd never been
afraid

It was then I realized the first chapter of life was to learn joy and
happiness
I walk with loneliness side-by-side
Swinging a short stick high in the air
Kicking dewdrops down the grassy trail on the outskirts of town

That night,
The constellations lovely and the frogs droned uncommonly loud
We let our guard down to soak in a pool of a clear creek as golden
sand rolled by
Suddenly, a thunderous crying sounded and a flash of lightning
whipped through the darkness

---

1 Ho-ee ho-ee (호이 호이) is onomatopoeia for a whistle.

In the next moment my body bleeding even as I realized my
struggles of desperation
I became aware that everything had gone away from me

At that moment in the second chapter of life, I learned of sorrow,
loneliness and grief
I walk with loneliness side-by-side
My robes like a flagstaff fluttering
Kicking dew down the grassy trail on the outskirts of town

The thin-thin thread of the net weaver unwinds
Something shoves me into the middle of a sea of solitude
Am I a helpless bit of broken ship?

I am pushed unceasingly
Toward the end of this sea of solitude
Am I a clamshell shoved and shoved into the sandy seaside?
Oh! In the sky all alone arms folded standing so—tall a dark—dark
shadow.......

고독 (孤獨)

나는 고독과 나란히 걸어간다
휘파람 호이호이 불며
교외(郊外)로 풀밭길의 이슬을 찬다

문득 옛일이 생각키움은 ── 그 시절이 조아졌음이라
뒷산 솔밭 속의 늙은 무덤 하나
밤마다 우리를 맞아 주었지만 어떠냐!

그때 우리는 단 한 번도
무덤 속에 무엇이 묻혔는 가를 알려고 해 본 적도 느껴 본 적도 없었다
떡갈나무 숲에서 부엉이가 울어도 겁나지 않았다

그 무렵 나는 인생의 제1과(第一課)를 즐겁고 행복한 것으로 배웠다
나는 고독과 나란히 걸어간다
하늘 높이 단장(短杖) 홰홰 내두르며
교외(郊外) 풀밭길의 이슬을 찬다

그 날 밤
성좌(星座)도 곱거니와 개고리 소리 유난유난 하였다
우리는 아무런 경계도 필요없이 금(金)모래 구르는 청류수(淸流水)에 몸을
담갔다
별안간 뇌성벽력(雷聲霹靂)이 울부짖고 번개불이 어둠을 채질했다
다음 순간 나는 내가 몸에 피를 흘리며 발악했던 것을 깨달었도
내 주위에서 모든 것이 떠나 갔음을 알았다

그때 나는 인생의 제2과(第二課)를 슬픔과 고적(孤寂)과 애수(哀愁)를
배웠나니
나는 고독과 나란히 걸어간다

깃폭인양 옷자락 펄펄 날리며
교외 풀밭길의 이슬을 찬다

낙사랑(絡絲娘)의 잣는 실 가늘게 가늘게 풀린다
무엇이 나를 적막(寂寞)의 바다 한가운데로 떠박지른다
나는 속절없이 부서진 배(船) 쪼각인가?

나는 대고 밀린다
적막(寂寞)의 바다 그 끝으로
나는 바닷가 사장(沙場)으로 밀려 밀려 나가는 조개 껍질인가?
오! 하늘가에 홀로 팔장끼고 우—뚝 선 저—거무리는 그림자여......

Goryeo Tomb

Those traces left by some person of old, who will recognize them
A hollowed out old tree, could you know its history
From time to time, coming to look for you
A cuckoo couple arrives to rest then leave together, were you even
aware?
(Goryeo To-o-omb Goryeo To-o-omb, only your name remains)

The rain, the wind harsh
The flow of time's turbulent watercourse gone, you should know
Even if skulls snore,
Even when the grave has vanished
What will be left behind in this empty place?
(Goryeo To-o-omb Goryeo To-o-omb, only your name remains)

Clearly, the person of this place
The things he wrote down in life
To guard this place as a symbol for countless years
Planted a banner of its proud history
Willfully hiding his body in this burial site, how many years have
passed?
(Goryeo To-o-omb Goryeo To-o-omb, only your name remains)

고려묘자 (高麗墓子)

옛님이 지나친 발자취 그 누가 알랴
속 비인 고목(古木) 너는 아느냐
때때로 너를 찾아와
쉬어가고 둘 다 가는 저_곽공(郭公)이나 아는가?
(꺼우리무_스 꺼우리무_스 네 이름만이 남었다)

비 바람 모질고
흘러간 세월의 물길 거칠어웠음을 알네라
해골들이 코 골든
뛰집(墓)마저 살아졌으니
무엇이 이 뒤으 빈터를 마르리?
(꺼우리무_스 꺼우리무_스 네 이름만이 남었다)

분명 님 이곳에서
지멀드록 써 너흐시다
그리다 이곳 변줄을 억만년 두고 직히려
자랑스러운 역사의 기치 꼽어두고
스스로 띄집 속에 몸을 숨기신지 그 몇 해?
(꺼우리무_스 꺼우리무_스 네 이름만이 남었다)

The Monologue of an Old Reed

The sun sets
The sparrows soon to sleep
The coots return from some unfamiliar rice paddy
When the wind comes to the village, at that time we speak sadly of
growing old

On the full moon
Together with a crab on a hill, watching the moon
With the river water, singing of time's passing
With shrimp sitting atop dried leaves, I enjoy such times

Which maid took my leaves to fashion adornments
Which child took my leaves to whistle with
Which wild goose took my stem and ran away
Ah, which Taegongmang[1] snatches away my youthfulness

This body measure by measure
Marked by lost love
Some star filled night, a reed-pipe in a riverboat passed by
Some rainy morning, a reed staff of a stranger came off the ferry
All these were my loves

An egret to my side
Dreamed of a baby water-snake on its back as it flew
A sickle returning from whetting to conquer me
Riding a cart deep into the mountains to be a reed mat to raise my
status

---

1   Taegongmang (태공망) was a Chinese noble who helped kings Wen and Wu of Zhou
    overthrow the Shang in ancient China. (Born 1128BC)

늙은 갈대의 독백

해가 진다
갈새는 얼마 아니하야 잠이 든다
물닭도 쉬이 어느 낯설은 논드렁에서 돌아온다
바람이 마을을 오면 그때 우리는 섧게 늙음의 이야기를 편다

보름달이면
갈거이와 함께 이 언덕에서 달보기를 한다
강물과 같이 세월의 노래를 부른다
새우들이 마른 잎새에 올라 앉느 이 때가 나는 좋다

어느 처녀가 내 잎을 따 갈부던 결었노
어느 동자가 내 잎닢 따 갈나발을 불었노
어느 기러기 내 순한 대를 입에다 물고 갔노
아, 어느 태공망이 내 젊음을 낚아 갔노

이 몸의 매듭매듭
잃어진 사랑의 허물 자국
별 많은 어느 밤 강을 날여간 강다릿배의 갈대 피리
비오는 어느 아침 나룻배 나린 길손의 갈대 지팽이
모두 내 사랑이었다

해오라비조는 곁에서
물뱀의 새끼를 업고 나는 꿈을 꾸었다
벼름질로 돌아오는 낫이 나를 다리려 왔다
달구지 타고 산골로 삿자리의 벼슬을 갔다

Autumn Colors

Isn't its rose-water smudged face beautiful

Isn't this red affection of a melting-ripe heart beautiful

This season, its autumn colors a bright crimson smile speaking in
scarlet

Is there sorrow in the passing wonder of youth

Does it dread being at the brink of dotage, of dying

As its aptitude abounds, the October sunlight blushes

Ripened by love at its peak the plump body of the leaf burns

The colors so proud and brilliant, even the blue-blue sky is dazzled

Autumn colors are the face of October, and the heart, but the
October foliage on the towering edge of cliff where two or three trees
feeling forsaken stand aslant, wavering

The colors of October are beautiful, but avoid loving them as even
crying could not blot out the resentment of reddish-purple

단풍 (丹風)

빨간 물 짙게 든 얼굴이 아름답지 않으뇨
빨간 정(情) 무르녹는 마음이 아름답지 않으뇨
단풍든 시절은 새빨간 웃음을 웃고 새빨간 말을 지줄댄다
어데 청춘靑春을 보낸 서러움이 있느뇨
어데 노사(老死)를 앞둘 두려움이 있느뇨
재화가 한끝 풍성하여 시월十月 햇살이 무색하다
사랑에 한창 익어서 살찐 띠몸이 불탄다
영화의 자랑이 한창 현란해서 청청한울이 눈부셔 한다
시월十月시절은 단풍이 얼굴이요, 또 마음인데 시월단풍도 높다란
낭떨어지에 두서너 나무 깨웃듬이 외로히 서서 한들거리는 것이 기로다
시월 단풍은 아름다우나 사랑하기를 삼갈 것이니 울어서도 다하지 못한
독한 원한이 빨간 자주로 지지우리지 않느뇨

Donkey

One morning, a bright day a warm wind blowing, in the village dogs barking and on the lane, kids running obliviously by, the once quiet village suddenly teeming.

This morning somewhere in the village in the dilapidated old forge at the corner of the garden the magpies call under the ash tree a traveler. The traveler with big ears black eyes having four short legs and wearing proper footwear.

Quietly its footfall quite like a large palm, the dark blue iron hoof's footfall pressed down.

Coming from some region this quiet-hearted traveler. Unloading bush clover and bamboo leaves flying off its mane, this traveler from some mountain district. It must be on the road returning from some distant mountain at a poor but peaceful house in the dim-light of daybreak in a shivering cold barn after eating green soybeans boiled with straw returning in the spreading haze through mountains and rivers near and far and all over the village to the feel of the sound of a cuckoo and clucking chickens.

Bound with the limbs of a withered tree, a painful nail digging in its sole, resigned to its nature it does not move as children throw stones and adults jeer hurling insults, his dignity intact looking at everything with pity taking it all in, all without the futility of blame, but just as a sad wretch alone in the empty field, yet with a heart full this traveler going to a distant market to sell morning bush clover and buy some food.

The day clear and the wind warm, this morning the traveler puts on painful new shoes and shoulders the bush clover, and as expected quietly leaves the village, crossing the bridge causing skylarks to take wing in the field and sending ducks soaring in the swamp

Alone in dreams and destiny as if for pleasure, as if in distaste, into the haze clump-clump plodding away on the long distant lane growing smaller.

당나귀

날은 밝고 바람은 따사한 어느 아츰날 마을에는 집집이 개들 짖고 행길에는 한물컨이 아이들이 달리고 이리하야 조용하든 마을은 갑자 기 흥성걸이었다.

이 아츰 마을 어구의 다 낡은 대장간에 그 마당귀 까치 짖는 마른 들메나무 아래 어떤 길손이 하나 있었다. 길손은 긴 귀와 껌언 눈과 짧은 네 다리를 하고 있어서 조릅하니 신을 신기우고 있었다.

조용하니 그 발에 모양이 자못 손바닥과 같은 검푸른 쇠자박을 대 이고 있었다.

그는 어늬 고장으로부터 오는 마음이 하도 조용한 손이든가. 싸리 단을 나려노코 갈기에 즉님새를 날리는 그는 어늬 산골로부터 오는 손이든가. 그는 어늬 먼 산골 가난하나 평안한 집 흰하니 먼동이 터오는 으스스하니 추운 외양간에서 조짚에 푸른콩을 삶어먹고 오는 길 이든가 그는 안개 어린 멀고 가까운 산과 내에 동네방네 뻑국이 소리 닭의 소리를 느껴웁게 들으며 오는 길이든가.

마른 나무에 사지를 동여매이고 그 발바닥에 아픈 못을 들여 백끼 우면서도 천연하야 움직이지 않고 아이들이 돌을 던지고 어른들이 비웃음과 욕사설을 퍼부어도 점잔하야 어지러히 하지 않고 모든 것을 다 가엽시 여기며 모든 것을 다 받어들이며 모든 것을 다 허물하거나 탓하지 않으며 다만 홀로 널따란 비인 벌판에 있듯이 쓸쓸하나 그러나 그 마음이 무엇에 넉넉하니 차 있는 이 손은 이 아츰 싸리단을 팔어 양식을 사려고 먼 장으로 가는 것이었다.

날은 맑고 바람은 따사한 이 아츰날 길손은 또 새로히 욕된 신을 신고 다시 싸리단을 짊어지고 예대로 조용히 마을을 나서서 다리를 건너서 벌에서는 종달새도 일쿠고 늪에서는 오리 떼도 날리며 홀로

제 꿈과 팔자를 즐기는 듯이 또 설어하는 듯이 그는 타박타박 아즈랑 이 낀 먼 행길에 작어저갔다.

The East Sea

Oh East Sea, this night so stifling I wear a straw hat and wander the street drinking bi-ru.[1] When you wear that straw hat and drink bi-ru while wandering the street, from somewhere, a somewhat sultry and salty piscine scent, oh East Sea, I suppose it comes from the fresh seaweed scattered at rocks rear along your seaside, this place of scattered seaweed as shore crabs hang about, sandpipers trill ssi-yang ssi-yang,[2] some maid in the village awaits another, and others like me drunk on soju laid out side by side on this sultry steaming night. Clearly, this fresh seaweed scent, must have been beached from the day's over-reaching water.

As I wear this straw hat, drinking bi-ru to the smell of fresh seaweed, oh East Sea, I would become your clam. When I am young a flower clam, when grown a surf clam, when old a puppy clam. Had I the energy, I would stick out my tongue biting shut, the water ten li deep below and me flying above. In the bright moonlight, I would want to be a moonflower distant from the seashore. On a night of a pitter-patter downpour, floating above the water singing 'Aewonseong,'[3] and in the warm tickle of a sunshiny morning, like a rice-washing wood bowl, I'll plunge and hoist from the seabed playing. Truth be told, I want to be a clam on the calm seabed lying in the soft sand to flirt about touching the heels of pretty maids who tread near and holding their hands.

Oh East Sea! As I wear this straw hat and drink bi-ru, there's a

---

1 Bi-ru (삐루) is the Japanese pronunciation for the word beer, which to Koreans was still foreign and uncommon, but trickled through from Japan to the Korean markets.

2 Ssi-yangssi-yang (씨양씨양) is Korean onomatopoeia for the high-pitched trill of a sandpiper.

3 Aewonseong (애원성 (哀怨聲)) is the name of a traditional Korean song literally entitled "The Sound of Sad Resentment" with a connotation of both love and hate.

friend who would know my mind of wanting to be a clam, who every night on an uninhabited island flock to rest atop a far-flung rock to lie, to sit, to chatter about the world and fall asleep, the seals. Though living in the ocean depths, he comes to the surface to breathe like a nobleman, when he dies he settles to the deep clutching a rock like a principled scholar, on occasion he tags along with gulls to play as an idler, as I like this friend I should come quickly to you before July arrives.

As I wear this straw hat drinking bi-ru and thinking of my dear friend, you always boast of your hairy crab with mung bean jelly,[4] such delicious side dishes. Indeed, as you well know under the Mansae Bridge at Hamheung in Hamgyeong province where you can taste the hairy crab, I alone live to open the woven blind.

Indeed, I cannot rule out that flatfish from those things I find familiar. Its flavor a fine fit for sashimi and cold noodles, fine in sikhye too.[5] Perch in bean paste stew's agreeable. Pollack soup, sea cucumber soup, fermented sweetfish, I'm proud of them all yet one thing you and I alone can see, how long the halfbeak's lower lip and Pacific pike's upper lip. Though it's not much to say, the raw abalone placed atop a trim and tidy blue reed mat, the taste of Hamgyeong soju shot by shot, if not for a Taoist hermit none would know.

Like this, when wearing a staw hat and drinking bi-ru, thinking of abalone and sea cucumber, something else comes to mind. In July or August, they say a boat from Jeju comes hanging with dark lamps on a yellowish background. Whenever the Jeju boat comes, the talk at your water's edge surges. The Jeju boat's auntie, built like a wood mortar, the uncle of the Jeju boat eats only millet rice and salt, something

---

4   Mung Bean Jelly (청포채) is a cloudy jelly made from mung beans and seasoned with a red pepper sauce.

5   Sikhye (식혜) is Hamgyeong dialect for a traditional Northern Korean side dish made with thin-sliced flatfish and chili powder.

happened to the Jeju boat's auntie as she picked sea cucumbers behind the rocks on the ridge one day...... Ah, such a commotion. When the Jeju boat comes ashore in the village, a welcome site, when the Jeju boat sets off so sorrowful. The children follow the Jeju boat along the waterfront, from a ridge the donkey lifts its eyes to follow.

This July, I'll go to you, get on the Jeju boat to live with some maid of Jeju.

As I wear a straw hat and drink bi-ru thinking all along of a Jeju maid, my heart goes back to that place, that smell of seaweed. Much as the clamshell grows rings, through the currents of time that maid grows year by year missing me, and you nearby a house smelling of pine resin where a man lives in grief after losing his wife, and that sharp-witted, four-year old Geum-i who spoke English so well, and you born in Dongsang village, in the township of Hongwon, Hongwon county, thinking of such things.

동해

동해여, 오늘밤은 이렇게 무더워 나는 맥고모자를 쓰고 삐루를 마시고
거리를 거닙네. 맥고 모자를 쓰고 삐루를 마시고 거리를 거닐면 어데서
넉넉한 비릿한 짠물 내음새 풍겨 오는데, 동해여 아마 이것은 그대의
바윗등에 모래장변에 날미역이 한불 널린 탓인가 본데 미역 널린 곳엔 방게가
어성기는가, 도요가 씨양씨양 우는가, 안마을 처녀가 누구를 기다리고 섰는가,
또 나와 같이 이 밤이 무더워서 소주에 취한 사람이 기웃들이 누웠는가.
분명히 이것은 날미역의 내음새인데 오늘 낮 물기가 쳐서 물가에 미역이 많이
떠들어 온 것이겠지.

이렇게 맥고모자를 쓰고 삐루를 마시고 날미역 내음새 맡으면 동해여,
나는 그대의 조개가 되고 싶읍네. 어려서는 꽃조개가, 자라서는 명주조개가,
늙어서는 강에지조개가. 기운이 나면 혀를 빼어 물고 물 속 십 리를 단숨에
날고 싶읍네. 달이 밝은 밤엔 해정한 모래장변에서 달바라기를 하고 싶읍네.
궂은 비 부슬거리는 저녁엔 물 위를 떠서 애원성이나 부르고, 그리고 햇살이
간지럽게 따뜻한 아침엔 이남박 같은 물바닥을 오르락내리락하고 놀고
싶읍네. 그리고 내가 정말 조개가 되고 싶은 것은 잔잔한 물밑 보드라운
세모래 속에 누워서 나를 쑤시러 오는 어여쁜 처녀들의 발뒤꿈치나 쓰다듬고
손길이나 붙잡고 놀고 싶은 탓입네.

동해여! 이렇게 맥고모자를 쓰고 삐루를 마시고 조개가 되고 싶어하는
심사를 알 친구가 하나 있는데, 이는 밤이면 그대의 작은 섬-사람 없는
섬이나 또 어느 외진 바위판에 떼로 몰려 올라서는 눕고 앉았고 모두들 세상
이야기를 하고 지껄이고 잠이 들고 하는 물개들입네. 물에 살아도 숨은 물
밖에 대고 쉬는 양반이고 죽을 때엔 물 밑에 가라앉아 바윗돌을 붙들고
절개 있게 죽는 선비이고 또 때로는 갈매기를 따르며 노는 활량인데 나는 이
친구가 좋아서 칠월이 오기 바쁘게 그대한테로 가야 하겠읍네.

이렇게 맥고모자를 쓰고 삐루를 마시고 친구를 생각하기는 그대의 언제나
자랑하는 털게에 청포채를 무친 맛나는 안주 탓인데, 정말이지 그대도 잘
아는 함경도 함흥 만세교 다리 밑에 님이 오는 털게 맛에 해가우손이를 치고
사는 사람입네.

하기야 또 내가 친하기로야 가재미가 빠질겝네. 회국수에 들어 일미이고
식혜에 들어 절미지. 하기야 또 버들개 봉구이가 좀 좋은가. 횃대 생선
된장지짐이는 어떻고. 명태골국, 해삼탕, 도미회, 은어젓이 다 그대 자랑감이지
그리고 한 가지 그대나 나밖에 모를 것이지만 공미리는 아랫주둥이가 길고
꽁치는 윗주둥이가 길지. 이것은 크게 할 말 아니지만 산뜻한 청삿자리
위에서 전복회를 놓고 함소주 잔을 거듭하는 맛은 신선 아니면 모를 일이지.
   이렇게 맥고모자를 쓰고 삐루를 마시고 전복에 해삼을 생각하면 또
생각나는 것이 있습네. 칠팔월이면 으레히 오는 노랑 바탕에 까만 둥을
단 제주 배 말입네. 제주 배만 오면 그대네 물가엔 말이 많아지지. 제주 배
아즈맹이 몸집이 절구통 같다는 둥, 제주 배 아뱅인 조밥에 소금만 먹는다는
둥, 제주 배 아즈맹이 언제 어느 모롱고지 이슥한 바위 뒤에서 혼자 해삼을
따다가 무슨 일이 있었다는둥……, 참 말이 많지. 제주 배 들면 그대네 마을이
반갑고 제주 배 나면 서운하지. 아이들은 제주 배를 물가를 돌아 따르고
나귀는 산등성에서 눈을 들어 따르지.
   이번 칠월 그대한테로 가선 제주 배에 올라 제주 색시하고 살렵네.
   내가 이렇게 맥고모자를 쓰고 삐루를 마시고 제주 색시를 생각하도 미역
내음새에 내 마음이 가는 곳이 있습네. 조개껍질이 나이금을 먹는 물살에
낱낱이 키가 자라는 처녀 하나가 나를 무척 생각하는 일과, 그대 가까이 송진
내음새 나는 집에 아내를 잃고 슬퍼 사는 사람 하나가 있는 것과, 그리고 그
영어를 잘하는 총명한 4년생 금이가 그대네 홍원군 홍원면 동상리에서 난
것도 생각하는 것입네.

Hair

Big aunt, your hair

Mama, your hair

Little aunt, your hair

When brushing your hair, all clumped in the comb

Big aunt, mama, and little aunt

Hair entangled in the eaves

Big aunt's hair entangled in the lower eaves

Mama's hairs entangled in the upper eaves

Little aunt's hair entangled in the upper eaves

Entangled in the eaves

Big aunt, mama, and little aunt

When clams come from the ocean over that mountain in early
spring

   Let's buy white clams, black clams, clams to cook on the fire pit and
eat

   Big aunt, mama, and little aunt

   Hair entangled in the eaves

   When the hairpin peddler comes from Hwang-hae in September or
October

   Let's buy a hairpin with thin needles and emerald Rubia

   In that event, how about some soft pink dye too

머리카락

큰마니야 네 머리카락
엄매야 네 머리카락
삼촌엄매야 네 머리카락
머리 빗고 빗덥에서 꽁지는 머리카락
큰마니야 엄매야 삼촌엄매야
머리카락을 텅납새에 끼우는 것은
큰마니 머리카락은 아룻간 텅납새에
엄매 머리카락은 웃칸 텅납새에
삼촌엄매머리카락도 웃칸 텅납새에
텅납새에 끼우는 것은
큰마니야 엄매야 삼촌엄매야
일은 봄철 산너머 먼 데 해변에서 가무래기 오면
힌가무래기 검가무래기 가무래기 사서 하리불에 구어 먹잔 말이로
구나
큰마니야 엄매야 삼촌엄매야
머리카락을 텅납새에 끼우는 것은
구시월 황하두서 황하당세 오면
막대심에 가는 세침 바늘이며 추월옥색 꼭두손이
연분홍 물감도 사잔 말이로구나

Epitaph
– Here Lies Juha Lee –

Born a poor son in Dancheon
His abilities outstanding
Reared studying at Yeongsang School
Then teaching at Yeongshin School
A pure and peaceful heart
Pleased the heavens and the people alike
With a willful mind, at twenty-three
Went to the East Sea
Our fellowship weeps

묘비명
–이주하 이 곳에 눕다–

가난한 아들로 단천에 나니
재간이 뛰어났다
자라 영생에 배우고
뒤에 영신에 가르칠쌔
맑고 고요한 마음이
하늘과 사람을 기쁘게 하였다
뜻을 두고 스물세 살로
동해에 가니
우리들의 정은 운다

Mountain District

Like a reed adornment, this mountain trail leads to the spring
The inns in numbers like hardy kiwi walking sticks

The stream flows with the sound of whining insects
Even in broad daylight on the mountain side
Cats wail like the flowing stream

The cows and horses return to the mountain
In the downpours, only the goats still cross the mountain brook's
bridge toward the hamlet

In the dark shade of a cliff in the morning
An owl flies heavily here
When the light of day comes, it flies away heavier

A child who came for the mineral spring from over the mountain
15-li distant, donning calabash gourds and in bush clover shoes, wet
with mountain rain

His father must be sick
Sick from eating Siberian gooseberry

In the village below the mountain, a baby shaman often performs
guts[1]

---

1   A gut (굿) is a ritual performed by a shaman involving offerings a sacrifices to the gods
    and ancestor worship for divination and healing.

산지

갈부던같은 약수터의 산거리
여인숙이 다래나무지팽이와 같이 많다

시냇물이 버러지소리를 하며 흐르고
대낮이라도 산옆에서는
승냥이가 개울물 흐르듯 울다

소와말은 도로 산으로 돌아갔다
염소만이 아직 된비가 오면 산개울에놓인다리를 건너 인가근처로 뛰어온다

벼랑탁의 어두운 그늘에 아츰이면
부헝이가 무거웁게 날러온다
낮이되면 더무거웁게 날러가버린다

산너머 십오리서 나무뒝치차고 싸리신신고 산비에촉촉이젖어서
약물을받으러오는 산아이도 있다

아비가 앓른가부다
다래먹고 앓른가부다

아랫마을에서는 애기무당이 작두를카며 굿을하는때가 많다

Winter Clothes

Winter clothes

Are they flower petals free from evil intentions?

Blooming only for a Taoist hermit living in the East

That young woman shamed the lonesome moon

That her hidden pearl was most admired by the sea

And she the shellfish

Resplendent with rich-crimson silk spread across the space, you are

that one woman

Is she originally from a different clan?

Her heart always burning like a silk comb in hand

Even all ablaze, burning bright

Her spirit neither green nor gleaming

Is a snow-hued gemstone

Purposely, hiding behind her back suddenly a strong will arose

Stealing a glance at a beautiful woman's heart from beyond a

mountain, the sun's burning passion

It's good that I can still sympathize

설의 (雪衣)

설의(雪衣)는
사념 없는 꽃잎이런가?
오직 신선이 사는 동방(東方)에서만 피고
그 젊은 여인은 달을 부끄릴 만큼 영롱한
진주알을 품은 이 바다가 가장 아끼여 마지않는
패류(貝類)로다
진홍금백(眞紅錦帛) 발 가득 펴 울장에 너는 한 여인이 있도다
그는 원래 우리의 종족이 다르냐?
그의 마음은 언제나 손에 든 비단빛처럼
활활 타며 있지만
그의 넋은 녹지도 연(戀)치도 않는 설색(雪色)의
광물질(鑛物質)이리라

짐짓 그의 등 뒤에 심지를 불끈 도두고
화미(華美)한 여심(女心)을 산 너머로 훔쳐보는 태양의 연정을
나는 동정해도 좋다

Acacia

Wounded by the falling frost, covering its feet with leaves, facing the azure sky spewing an incessant chill wind as if dead an Acacia stands tall

Without pretense or posturing its dark torso persists. But not so lazy as to harden or be armed and to its chest yellow birds wing and wait on its branches in the style of a girl weeping shik- shik-[1] but he remains a rock unconcerned.

Indeed through ten thousand years living abundantly
A future of one hundred million years!
As if it will live one hundred million years into the future

On the knoll, one distinguished acacia digging root, standing in the heart of time and space, resigned to life and history, today and yesterday.

1 Shik- shik- (씩- 씩-) the sound of an
indignant woman's bitter crying.

아카시아

서리에 상해 떨어진 체 입사귀로 발치를 묻고 쉴새 없이 찬 바람을
토애해는 창공과 마주쳐 죽은 듯이 우뚝 선 아카시아

아무런 가식도 허세도 꾸미지 않은 검은 몸이로다. 그러나 몸에 굳
거나 무장하기를 게을리 아니하고 가슴패기 노란 누릅치기 몇 마리
날러와 가지에 머므르고 소녀같은 맵시로 애련한 목소리 내여 씩- 씩-
울지만 그는 오직 바위 같이 둔감하다.

가왕 만년을 복히 살어왔고
장차 억년을!
장차 억년을 더 살리라는 듯

둔덕 위에 쟁쟁한 아카시아 한 그루 시공을 헤집고 그 한복판에서 서
서 생과 역사를 오늘도 어제도 체념하다.

Mother's Parents' Place

My mother's parents' place where I'm always afraid

When early evening arrives, the inner court crowds with white-whiskered Siberian weasels, converging and in close concert, crying harsh jjyang-jjyang jjyang-jjyang[1]

At night, something throws scores of stones to the tiled roof and runs away to the pear tree at the fence in the back, someone wears a lamp tied by a string, something took out big pots, small pots, everything from the wood-burning stove and scattered them all around, the person who went to the outhouse as a consequence had his neck held and thrown harshly in the hole

Then at dawn, on a store room rack, stacks and stacks of wooden bowls, big wooden trays, rice cake platters and containers scatter on the floor, such a house

---

1 Jjyang-jjyang (쨩쨩 쨩쨩) is onomatopoeia the short, sharp bark of excited weasels.

외가집

내가 언제나 무서운 외가집은

초저녁이면 안팎마당이 그득하니 하이얀 나비수염을 물은 보득지근한
복족제비들이 씨글씨글 모여서는 쨍쨍 쨍쨍 쇳스럽게 울어대고

밤이면 무엇이 기왓골에 무릿돌을 던지고 뒤울안 배나무에 쩨듯하니 줄등을
헤여달고 부뚜막의 큰 솥 적은 솥을 모주리 뽑아놓고 제통(뒷간)에 간 사람의
목덜미를 그냥그냥 나려 눌려선 잿다리 아래고 처박고

그리고 새벽녘이면 고방 시렁에 채국채국 얹어둔 모랭이 목판 시루며
함지가 땅바닥에 넓너른히 널리는 집이다.

Wollim Market[1]

Where the 'Eight Kilometers Northeast to HeeCheon' signpost
stands
Near a stone-shingled house, an oxcart, straw shoes, an old
wardrobe
Near some mountain stream, quack-quack a cocksure pheasant cries

On the ninth day of the month at the market
A wild mountain boar, a family of raccoons, a 'twi-twi' thrush
appear
And hazelnuts, oats, acorn jelly,[2] and thick acorn porridge appear[3]

I buy fist-sized hunks of rice cake and taffy sweeter than honey
And as if awash in yellow's intensity, the bold yellow-smear under
late autumn's sunlight in some secluded mountain district
Rubbing that bright, bold yellow millet[4] until my eyes dazzled
Preferring those rice cakes, mixed rice, and alcohol made from
millet
And thinking of that the delicious millet-pumpkin soup, I am glad

1   Wollim (월림(月林)장) is the name of a small village or hamlet in Pyeongan Bukdo.

2   Dotori-muk (도토리묵) is an acorn jelly used as a Korean side dish.

3   Bumbuk (범벅) a mixture representing a variety of dishes in which something (often
    rice) is mixed with a powder to make porridge.

4   Haetgijangssal (햇기장쌀) in Korea is a type of millet called proso millet, prickly millet,
    or watergrass.

월림(月林) 장

자시동북팔십희천(自足東北八十熙川)의 표(標)말이 선 곳
돌능와집에 소달구지에 싸리신에 옛날이 사는 장거리에
어니 근방 산천(山川)에서 덜걱이 꿱꿱 검방지게 운다

초아흐레 장판에
산 멧도야지 너구리가족 튀튀새 낫다
또 가얌에 귀이리에 도토리묵 도토리범벅도 낫다

나는 주먹다시 가튼 떨광이에 꿀보다도 달다는 강낭엿을 산다
그리고 물이라도 들 듯이 샛노라티 샛노란 산(山)골 마가을 벼테
눈이 시울도록 샛노라티 샛노란 햇기장쌀을 주물으며
기장쌀은 기장찻떡이 조코 기장차랍이 조코 기장감주가 조코 그리
고 기장쌀로 쑨 호박죽은 맛도 잇는 것을 생각하며 나는 기뿌다

List of Onomatopoeia

꺼우리무—스 (ggeo-u-ri-mu-seu)
Goryeo To-o-omb, with a ghostlike
lingering ooh to the word tomb

꽁꽁 (ggong-ggong)
frozen solid or frozen stiff

너슬너슬 (neo-seul neo-seul)
dialect for 너울너울 (neo-ul neo-ul)
waveringly, swaying or billowing

다문다문 (da-mun da-mun)
dialect for deumun deumun (드문드문),
sparsely or thinly scattered

데굴데굴 (daegol daegol)
a mimetic word for round and rolling

들썩들썩 (deul-sseok deul-sseok)
up and down, clamorous and noisy,
riotous, shrill and sharp, spirited sound

매딥매딥 (mae-dib mae-dib)
measure by measure

무럭무럭 (mu-reok mu-reok)
plume, grow, or rise and swell

물씬물씬 (mul-ssin mul-ssin)
strongly scented

부숭부숭 (bu-soong bu-soong)
downy and dry

삐삐 (bbi-bbi)
the sound of boiling, bubble-bubble,
also mimetic for gaunt

악악 (ag-ag)
the caw-caw squawk of a waterbird

비애고지 (bi-ae-go-ji)
the tweet, trill and twitter, chitter-
chatter of swallows

사르릉 쪼로록 (sa-reu-reung jjo-ro-
rok) the sound of urination
tinkle and trickle, dribble and drop

쇠리쇠리 (soe-ri soe-ri)
shiny, glaring or bright

스르럭 스르럭 (seu-re-rok seu-re-rok)
the swish-swish of flap & flutter

쌀랑쌀랑 (ssal-rang ssal-rang)
pat pat or pitter-patter, plip-plop

씨굴씨굴 (ssi-gol ssi-gol)
a soft murmuring sound, constant coos

짱짱짱짱 (jjang jjang jjang jjang)
the sound of ice splitting and cracking

채국채국 (chae-gug chae-gug)
piled neatly, trim and tidy

씩- 씩- (shik- shik-)
sob sob, sniff sniff or bawl and blubber

씨양씨양 (ssi-yang ssi-yang)
the high-pitched trill of a sandpiper

오독독이 탕탕 (o-dok-dok-i tang-
tang) fireworks blazing, burst and pop

욱실욱실 (wook-sil wook-sil)
maggot-like, squirming

응성응성 (woong-seong woong-seong)
abuzz in the hubbub, mixed in murmur

응앙응앙 (eung-ang eung-ang)
a donkey's call, hee-haw hee-haw

졸레졸레 (jol-rae jol-rae)
mimetic, following around, row by row

지중지중 (ji-joong ji-joong)
thoughtfully, pensive, wistful, musing
and meditatively, with lapping thoughts

짱짱 짱짱 (jjyang-jjyang jjyang-jjyang)
the short, sharp bark of excited weasels

짜랑짜랑 (jjarang jjarang)
a repetative jinlging sound, jing-jingling

쩌락쩌락 (jjeo-rag jjeo-rag)
the sound of a wooden mallet striking
dough when making Korean rice cakes

쩜벙쩜벙 (jjeom-beong jjeom-beong)
a spirited splash and spray

쩔쩔 (jjeol jjeol)
to sip and slurp

챙챙 (chaeng-chaeng)
clear and clean, sunshiny

촉촉이 (chok-chok-ee)
damp, wet, or doused

츠렁츠렁 (cheu-reong cheu-reong)
a mimetic word for long hair hanging
down

찌륵찌륵 (jjiruk jjiruk)
the sound of slurping

캥캥 (kaeng-kaeng)
barking, yap and yelp

쾅쾅 (kwang-kwang)
the sound of a drum, thump and thud

뿡뿡 (bboong-bboong)
sound of a boat whistle blowing, toot
and blast

타박타박 (ta-bak ta-bak)
a mimetic word for plodding along,
clump clump, tramp and tromp

터벅터벅 (teo-beok teo-beok)
mimetic for crunching along, stepping in
snow

푹푹 (puk-puk)
mimetic for the accumulation of snow

호이호이 (ho-ee ho-ee)
the sound of whistling

유난유난 (yu-nan yu-nan)
droning, uncommonly loud

흥성흥성 (heung-seong heung-seong)
crowded and booming, teeming and
bursting with energy, a growing din

Chronology

Baek Seok's Timeline 白石 시인 연보 (年譜)

1912

Born July 1ˢᵗ in Pyunganbukdo province, Jungju city to father Baek Shi Bak 백시박 (白時璞) and mother Lee Bong Woo이봉우(李鳳宇) as Baek Gi Haeng (also known as Gi Yun). Although Baek Seok 백석(白石, 白奭) was his pen name, he principally went by it in everyday activities after the age of 19. In his early days, his father was a section leader in photography at the Ilmuro (now Chosun Ilbo) newspaper, but left to return home to Jungju to run a lodging house.

1918
6 years old

Entered Osan primary school

1924
12 years old

Began Osan school. According to his classmates, he envied the poet Kim Sowol (김소월), his upperclassman, so Baek Seok developed a deep interest in literature and Buddhism.

1929
17 years old

Graduated from the Osan school.

1930
18 years old

Applied to the Chosun Ilbo literary contest with the novelette "The Mother and Son" [그 모(母)와 아들] and won the prize, thereby embarking on his literary career. In March, he was awarded a scholarship with the support of the Chosun Ilbo and he went to study in Japan. Attending Aoyama school in Tokyo, he studied English literature. He also developed a discussion with fellow scholarship winner Jang Geun Yang (정근양). At that time, he became infatuated with the work of the popular Japanese poet, Ishikawa Takobuko (石川啄木) and took on his pen name.

1934
22 years old

Graduated Aoyama school and returned to Seoul to work as a reporter and journalist for the Choson Ilbo delving into the lifestyle of Seoul. Also worked in the publishing department of an affiliated magazine, Yeoseong 〈여성(女性)〉 as an editor. And through the Choson Ilbo translated foreign works and theses.

1935
23 years old

Published "Jungju Fortress" [정주성(定州城)] on August 31st while reporting for the Choson Ilbo and began devoting himself more to producing poetry. Worked on the publishing team of the literary magazine, Bright Morning 〈조광(朝光)〉

1935
23 years old

Sometime in June at his friend Ho Joon's wedding announcement dinner, to his life's relief he met the woman Ran. At the time a student at Ewha Woman's High School. They lived together in the Fall of the following year.

1936
24 years old

Jan, 20th published a 100 copy limited edition of his short collection, "Deer" {사슴} at Sungwang Printing Corp. On Jan. 29th held a ceremony of publication at the Seoul TaeSo Hall 태서관(太西館). The hosts of this Promotion ceremony were Ahn SukYoung, Ham TaeHoong, Hong KiMoon, Kim

KyuTaek, Lee WonJo, Lee KapSup, Moon TongPyo, Kim Haekyun, Shin HyunJoon, Ho Joon, and Kim KiRim , all together 11 people. The same year in April, resigned from the Chosun Ilbo and went to Hamheung city in HamKyung South Province to teach English at YoungSang High School. Afterwards, published the essays "Flatfish" and "Donkey" in the DongAh Ilbo about his impressions of life. At about the same time, he met the kisaeng, Kim Jin Hyang at the Choson Kisaeng call office and fell in love with her. He then gave her the nom de plume Jaya [자야(子夜)] meaning the time between 11pm and 1am.

1937
25 years old

While teaching at YoungSang High School, he often went to a store managed by a Russian to learn Russian. Being pressed from his hometown to marry, he returned but left after the nuptial ceremony for Hamheung to live with Jaya. However, Jaya learned the truth and fled for Seoul alone. Published the five poem collection, "Poems of a trip to Hamju" 〈함주시초(咸州詩抄)〉

1938
26 years old

Coached YoungSaeng High School's soccer team and led his players to matches all around Korea. At this time, he was reunited with Jaya. The soccer players visited a tavern and caused trouble so Baek Seok was censured by the school association and asked to transfer to YoungSaeng Girls' School. He resigned and returned to Seoul to edit Yeoseong.

1939 27 years old	Was again married but returned to Seoul alone. When Jaya learned of this, she again abandoned him. On Jan. 26th he again participated as editor of Yosong and resigned on Oct. 21st. He took a trip to near his hometown in Pyunganbukdo and told his friends HyoJun and Jeong Hyeon Woong (허준과 정현웅) "I will go to the wide plains of Manchu and bring a hundred poems" and with this resolve, later in the year, moved to Shinkyung [now JungChun 장춘(長春)], Manchuria, where he resided at the Shiyoung House in Mr. Hwang's room.
1940 28 years old	While working in the economic bureau, was pressed to change his name to a Japanese surname but refused. He then traveled to the remote parts of northern Manchu where he made contact with a primitive tribe and subsequently broadened his geographical and spiritual perspective. He then wrote the criticism "Sadness and Truth" for the Manchu–Chosun Ilbo. Baek Seok hosted the ceremony of publication for the poet Pak PilYang's (박팔양) "Yosu Shicho" 〈여수시초(麗水詩抄)〉. Made friends with the poets of Manchu, Kim SaRyang, Bak PalYang, Song JiYoung, and An Mak. Translated and published Thomas Hardy's "Tess of the D'Urbervilles" and briefly returned to Seoul for this reason. Having much trouble finding housing, he then shared his cave-like room with his friend Lee HyungJu (이형주).

1941 29 years old	Eked out an existence as a surveying assistant, secretary and tenant farmer.
1942 30 years old	Worked as a customs official. Translated the work of Russian writer Nikolai Apollonovich Baikov.
1944 32 years old	Hid in the remote mountains working at a mine to avoid the Japanese forced draft for wartime workers.
1945 33 years old	Following Korea's liberation, moved for a short stay in Shineuiju and then returned to his hometown of Jungju and worked in an orchard.
1946 34 years old	At the request of Cho ManShik, came to Pyeongyang to work as translating secretary in the Korean Democratic party. According to Go Jeong Hun, when his son died in transit from Manchu, he went to see Baek Seok in Pyeongyang where he was living with a kisaeng.
1947 35 years old	Through his friend Ho Jun (허준), the poem "Silent Land" 〈적막강산〉 was published in New World Magazine. With the division of Korea, all his poetry was buried and forgotten in the South.
1948 36 years old	It was reported that he lectured in English and Russian at Kim IlSung University.

1949 37 years old	Translated and published Scholohof's (숄로호프) "Silent River Don" and "They Fought for their Motherland." According to Go Jeong Hun's (고정훈) account, Baek Seok had a wife who had graduated from Ewha School who hated him so she fled South with his only son and threatened bodily harm if he followed her.
1950 38 years old	When soldiers reclaimed Pyunganbukdo, the residents recommended him as mayor of Jungju county.
1953 41 years old	Translated and published "Pablanko's Happiness" 〈행복〉.
1954 42 years old	Translated and published selected poems of Norminsy Asakofsky.
1956 44 years old	Became interested in children's literature and wrote the essay "For the Development of Fairytales" 〈동화문학의 발전을 위하여〉.
1957 45 years old	Wrote a fairytale The Four Crab Brothers 〈집게네 네 형제〉
1958 46 years old	Presented poetry critique "Thoughts on Socialist Morality."
1959 47 years old	Until this time living in Pyeongyang near Tongdaewon Station, dedicated himself to the translation and creation of Russian novels and poetry under the auspices of the Korean

Writers' Alliance at the Central Committee's Foreign
Literature Translation Office – according to the Donga
Ilbo 04/30/2001. Published seven poems including "Early
Spring" in Chosun Literature Magazine.

1960
48 years old

In December of this year, published two poems including
Farewell in Chosun Literature magazine

1961
49 years old

In December, published his last three poems including "A
Man who Returned" in Chosun Literature magazine. His
life after this date could not be verified and it was thought
he was likely the the victim of a purge in the North.

1963
51 years old

It was rumored that he had passed away.

1987
75 years old

His first collection, "Deer and Other Poems" totaling 94
poems were arranged, "Baek Seok's Collected Poetry"
compiled and edited by Lee Dong Soon was issued by the
Creation and Review Publishing House (창작과비평사). At
that time the ban on writers who went North (월북자가)
was lifted.

The books "The Evening the Newlywed Pak Came" and
"Baek Seok's Collected Works" were published by Saemoon
Publishing House.

1988 76 years old	Kim, Jaya presented her retrospective entitled "Baek Seok, A Name I Cannot Erase from My Heart" in Creation and Review Publishing House's magazine
1989 77 years old	"Baek Seok's Poetry Woman of Gajeurang" issued by Saemoon Publishing House.
1990 78 years old	"Baek Seok's Poetry A White Wind Wall" issued by Koryowon Publishing House.
	"The Sound of Wild Birds" selected poems issued by Mirae Publishing House.
1994 82 years old	Compiled data on Baek Seok and through Jina Publishing House issued "The Poet Baek Seok's Biography" in two volumes.
1995 83 years old	SongJoon again published the two volume "Baek Seok's Biography" and "Baek Seok's Collected Poems" through Hakyoung Publishing House.
	"Baek Seok My Love" written by Kim Jaya was issued by Munhak Dongnae Publishing House.
1996 83 years old	Baek Seok died in January at the age of 83.

"Simple celebrations of traditional rural life, tastes, smells, sounds of the countryside dominate the poems of this romantic, solitary figure. Anyone curious to discover a Korean poet who maintained a deep love for older Korean life-experience need look no further."

-- *Brother Anthony of Taizé, Sogang University*

"The unique temporal exoticism characterizing the early phase of Baek Seok's poetry is exquisitely caught in this version. The pervading sense of existential pathos and loneliness in his Manchu Poems would never cease to appeal. An unflinching outsider, the poet in a destitute time, at last, came to find a reliable foreign fellow traveler."

-- *Professor Yu Jongho, Yonsei University*

THANK YOU FOR READING!

Want a FREE audio book sample?
Just sign up for our VIP mailing list for updates, new releases and exclusive promotions at koreanpoets.org/bonus and we'll send you audio of poems from Baek Seok's only published collection, Deer, as a special gift.

If you enjoyed the poems in this book, please go to Amazon, Kyobo or your favorite online bookstore to write a brief recommendation. Every review helps! Also, go to exilepress.com to check out other outstanding books by Exile Press and its imprints.